THE 4TH MARKING PERIOD

A Memoir of an African American Male Guidance Counselor

Richard L. Wilson, Jr., MA

authorHOUSE®

AuthorHouse™
1663 Liberty Drive, Suite 200
Bloomington, IN 47403
www.authorhouse.com
Phone: 1-800-839-8640

First published by AuthorHouse 9/22/2008

ISBN: 978-1-4389-1918-8 (sc)

Printed in the United States of America
Bloomington, Indiana

This book is printed on acid-free paper.

This book is dedicated to my wife Stacey, my father & mother Rev. and Mrs. Richard L. Wilson, Sr., my sister Cheryl, Jacki, all of my family members (especially my cousin Lisa who encouraged me to write down my day-to-day feelings and make a book out of them), my church family (Bethel UHC), my special "circle of friends" that have encouraged me in all my endeavors, the brothers of Alpha Phi Alpha Fraternity, Inc. especially my line brothers from *The 12 Disciples* Fall 1989, all of my mentors in my life, and to all of the youth I have worked with throughout my years as a counselor, therapist, and guidance counselor.

Special thanks to my fraternity brother and entertainment lawyer James Walker, Esq., my graduate school advisor Dr. E. Ahia, (I am still waiting for my steak dinner), and to Mr. Douglas Lehnert for editing my first book.

To withhold the identities of the students and staff, the names mentioned in this book are fictitious.

FOREWORD

The 4th Marking Period: A Memoir of an African American Male Guidance Counselor is a day to day account of a Guidance Counselor who is overwhelmed by a task that he feels he is called to do. This text, however, alludes to several deeper themes that plague American education. Researchers have pointed out that our education systems should recognize the need for collaboration among professionals in our educational communities. Mr. Wilson's feeling alone in his efforts, in part, suggests the same need. Staff should feel free to express concerns without feeling intimidated or scorned. Staff should be given a safe place to confess biases without being labeled. This brand of honest transparency will break down barriers that appear in this case, to prevent collaborated success for the students. Another underlying issue revealed in this text is the frustration most education professionals feel when they are unable to tap into the causes for the symptoms of underachievement among students. These memoirs open the door for genuine self-examination of why one goes into education, what continued professional development should be employed, and a genuine evaluation of systemic problem solving. This honest account of one's feelings should be a beginning to open dialogue that would result in genuine help for the students and professional development for those involved. This open and honest assessment of the situation and portrayal of ones feelings lends itself to the next phase, earnest pursuit of solutions and deliberate application for the advancement of the students that this concerned African American Male Guidance Counselor has portrayed.

Mrs. Glyndora King, MA
Retired School Teacher

INTRODUCTION

I was inspired to take some of my journal entries and transform them into a book. From March 2 to May 4, 2008, I will give you the reader an idea of what I go through in a typical work day. You will also experience my thoughts and feelings as an African American man working in the school system. It is challenging! I titled this book *The 4th Marking Period* because most of the journal entries are from during the fourth marking period at my school. Thank God! This is <u>NOT</u> a "how-to" book. This <u>WILL NOT</u> give you counseling tips or techniques on how to deal with middle school students. I know how to use techniques that were taught to me from a textbook in my classes in college, but to tell you the truth, some of my techniques are unorthodox. You may laugh or you may frown at how I respond to students; however, if you ask any student in my school who Mr. Wilson is you will get a <u>positive</u> response.

This book does not put on display my skills as a counselor; it does however give you a taste of my thoughts, feelings, and reactions to certain situations I encounter in my school. Some of the things I say in this book express my feelings as an African American man. Some of my opinions may be harsh to you as readers but they are the truth and I know there are other Black men who feel the same way. I am a kind-hearted, easy-going, occasionally moody man who loves working with youth, especially my students. I treat every student differently. I joke and laugh with some and I am serious and to the point with others. I have learned with whom I can joke and with whom I can't. I know which students need the extra push and the students who need to be left alone. Nonetheless, I try to speak to and get to know every student that comes in this building, especially our African American students.

Even with parents, with some I am very blunt and straight to the point, and for others I give them what they want to hear. When it comes to certain issues, such as suicide ideation, the loss of a family member or close friend, or conflict resolution, to name a few, there are standard counseling techniques, policies and procedures that I must follow.

Look, just in case you want to question my credibility, I have had many years of schooling, earning a BA and Master's degree that have taught me what I should do. I do believe however that this generation of children needs more than what is presented in books. Overall, I believe we are dealing with a violent, non-mannered, selfish, low academically skilled, heavily influenced by television, opinionated not factual, disrespectful to parents and adults, sexually promiscuous, video game generation. Who is to blame? The school? The parents? Society? I don't know.

In any case, you are about to enter the mind of a African American male guidance counselor who wants to address these critical issues.

I believe I was called to work with our youth. I don't do it for the money. I can remember my first job out of college was a counselor at a runaway shelter making $16,000 a year sometimes working six days a week and double shifts. I have been working with youth for over fifteen years. I owe it to my family, my fraternity, and the many role models who encouraged me to work with our youth to do this.

I can remember when I decided I wanted to pursue a career in counseling. It came to me like a ghost in the night. During my college days I remember talking to female students about their ex-boyfriends who did not treat them well. I was the shoulder to cry on. Of course, I had a hidden agenda, (what brother didn't in college?), I was considered the "sensitive brotha" especially to the needs of other people. I was the one who listened and gave good advice not knowing at that time that it was my destiny to become a counselor, therapist, or mental health professional.

My first "real" job as a counselor was with a runaway shelter for abused children. During that time in my life, my eyes where opened to the cruelty and maltreatment of children as young as five. I remember I had a case of a five year old African American boy who took care of himself. His mother was a heroin user, he didn't know his father, and the grandmother was a chronic alcoholic. We picked him up drinking out of a puddle in the middle of the street. When he stayed at the shelter, he would sleep on the cold floor and we would have to wake him up by shouting from the doorway because he reacted violently if we tried to get him up physically.

I was transferred to a transitional living program where I was an overnight counselor, while working a part-time graduate assistantship and going to school full-time for my Master's in counseling. For ten years I worked diligently in the social services arena. I worked as a therapist in group homes, detention centers (adult and juvenile), drug treatment programs, and I even worked at Planned Parenthood as an HIV Counselor.

I vividly remember one day they were short on staff downstairs in the clinic department at Planned Parenthood and I had to do pregnancy options counseling. Wow! That was an experience because the client stared at me for at least thirty seconds. Imagine a young Black male counselor talking with a pregnant white middle-aged female! Yeah, I was young. I earned my master's degree when I was twenty-four years old. She was, however, very interested in what I had to say. After the session, she said, "Rich I was very comfortable with you..." Years passed by as I switched from job to job in social services. Then I entered the realm of Education.

My first year in the school system was tough. Basically, let me start my journey by saying it was rumored around the school that "he won't last!" Well this is five years later and I am tenured. I can't complain because I am truly thankful about having a job. I feel that I am blessed with a supportive administration. Sometimes, however, I am faced with challenges that only Black men go through and it seems like no one understands them.

My mind and heart are laced with integrity, character, and determination, but my blood is laced with pain and anger for the treatment of Black men in America and the "invisibility" we experience in the workplace, society, and sometimes in our relationships. In this book, I only share a small percentage of what I may go through in a given day at my school. Visualize in your own mind what is about to unfold in this journey in the life of an African American male guidance counselor during the 4th marking period.

Sunday, March 2, 2008

It's Sunday evening and I am actually dreading going to work. It is not because I am mistreated, but because I feel invisible; like I am not even there. I try to be outgoing but I know I am the topic of conversation being the only African American male on professional staff in the building besides my venting buddy, our custodian of twenty something years (the other brother from another mother.) For example, during my first year a teacher informed me that the other counselors were talking about me and how they "are not here to train anyone", (anyone meaning me.) I was constantly watched however, to see what I would do in certain situations. Some staff speak, some don't unless they need something.

The kids love me though. Why? They probably haven't seen a positive, well-spoken, Black man who can identify with their culture. Yes, I try to keep up with these kids. I want to know what they know, what they listen to, what they like and don't like, who is their boyfriend or girlfriend this week, whom they want to fight, who are their friends for now, what's the new IM and texting lingo, I want to know EVERYTHING! They know my "yes" is yes and my "no" is no, and that I will call their parents or parent or guardian in a heartbeat, (you have to be careful nowadays… having both parents in the home is almost obsolete).

I coached eighth grade basketball this year. Our record was 8-2! Well, let me tell the truth, it was 2-8. Yeah, I had a losing season my first year coaching. The players liked me but they didn't like me. Why? Academics and professionalism came first.

I can remember my high school basketball career. It was my junior season and I was starting varsity. I made the local newspaper a few times. I played power forward and I was a pretty good player. Then one day, I came home with a D in trigonometry on my report card. My dad came to the game and told the coach that this was my last game. "I don't allow D's in my house." Back then I was furious! Today, I am thankful.

My students/players had to wear ties on game day and they had progress reports weekly! Yes, I was a imitation Coach Carter (didn't get a movie made about me though). Of course the team and some parents blamed the losing season on me. "The coach doesn't know what he's doing!" "He sucks as a coach!" Yeah maybe, but I'm educated! I have a retirement fund! I have two degrees and I'm working on a third! Don't put the blame on me, I was trying to teach these boys how to succeed on and off the court. Anyway, it was a good season and I enjoyed it. My cousin said I looked like an NBA coach. I was inspired to develop a basketball program and I am implementing it next year. Well let me go get mentally ready for tomorrow.

Monday, March 3, 2008

It is Monday morning. The closer I walked towards the school the more I disappeared. Man, four months to go before I get a summer break. This year has been up and down for me. Sometimes, I hate being the only black man here besides our custodian. Sometimes I dread coming to work because I know I have to deal with situations no one else will ever experience. If some of you did not get that, basically, I have to keep smiling and not appear hostile or I will lose my job. I am the only African American in the front office and sometimes it's hard for me mentally. You know I was talking to one of the teachers and they stated "you know, the kids need you here..." Why? To destroy the image that BET, the media, and the newspapers display regarding Black men. What can a brother do? Well I guess I'd better get to work.

Tuesday, March 4, 2008

"Back in the Hole again." It was hard for me to come in. I feel no one knows what it is like to be me. We had a staff meeting yesterday and I felt invisible. I felt alone. I just sat there and read a book. I try to tell these young Black male students here in the school that life is going to deal them a bad hand, if they haven't been dealt a bad hand already. They looked at me as if I was

2

smoking crack! I get a little upset when they appear not to care. Our young Black men are in a state of crisis. SOMEBODY HELP! PLEASE! I can't really think right now so I am going to end it here.

Wednesday, March 5, 2008

Today I know it is going to be challenging because I am so very tired. Going to the gym at 5 a.m. is taking a toll on me and I am not getting any younger. I actually dozed off while I was typing! What does the day hold for me today? I wish I was in a nice warm bed.

I feel as though I am getting sick. I have to build up my immune system to work around these students. The students at my school will just cough in the air, hack, sneeze, and just do so many "dirty" things. Children today lack basic manners.

I was on the phone and a student decided to walk right in and sit in a chair in my office. I told the person on the other end of the phone to hold on and I let that student have it! I told him to get up and not come back until he got some manners. Whom do I blame?

I believe the parents need to start being parents. Parents are no longer in control, the children are. One child told her mother "Get the F*** out of my room!" Oh no! After the swelling from the knot on her head went down, I would have called DYFS on myself! Another girl locked herself in her room and the parent called me to ask what he should do. HUH? I told him to take the door off the hinges and inform his daughter that it goes back on when she pays rent, groceries, and part of the phone bill. Children are not adults they are CHILDREN!

Thursday, March 6, 2008

It's Thursday morning and the weekend is almost here. I should call out tomorrow. I can't because I called out last Friday. I am a funny dude. You know we as Black men, need sick days for both medical and mental health days. We need to clear our minds from everything that's going on.

I was in a dilemma yesterday as a counselor. Two students came down to my office to settle a conflict. One of the students was very upset because the other student made a derogatory statement about Puerto Ricans. "Mr. Wilson he called me a dumb Puerto Rican..." The white student claimed that the other student called him a "cracker" and a "wigger." What is a 'wigger?' I said to both students that they were making this into a race issue. Just stop! But here is what kills me... both students are supposed to be best friends! Huh? I told the students that I would say nothing to hurt my friend, especially making derogatory racial comments.

Wait... Here comes my Vice Principle, something must have happened...

I have a student in my office now who decided to punch another student in the chest for no reason. First, I informed the student not to lie, that honesty is the policy. Second, I told him to realize that there are certain things you can and cannot do in school. He stated that he was "playing around." The other student is in the nurse's office claiming he needs to go to the hospital because of chest pains. I just took a deep breath.

The student sitting in my office is worried, BIG TIME! "Are you going to call my mom?" he asks in a quivery voice.

"Yup." No discussion, no explanation. "Your mother needs to know how you are playing around in school." The challenge is whether or not I can get in touch with his mother. His father has no involvement (as usual for most young Black boys), therefore mom, who works two jobs just to make ends meet to feed the student and his younger brother, has to take off work to come and get him... Life.

Friday, March 7, 2008

IT'S FRIDAY! I was reading this article yesterday about overcoming invisibility. It seems as though everyone today suffers from some sort of disorder – ADHD, ADD, Depression, Anxiety, Anorexia... I suffer from Invisibility Syndrome as defined by Dr. Anderson J. Franklin in his book *From Brotherhood to Manhood: How Black Men Rescue Their Relationships and Dreams from the Invisibility Syndrome.* In Ralph Ellison's book *The Invisible Man* (which I read in college not knowing at that time that I would become invisible later in life) he defines what it means to be invisible: *"I am a man of substance, of flesh and bone... I am invisible; understand, simply because people refuse to see me... They see only my surroundings, themselves, or figments of imagination... indeed, everything and anything except me."*

I feel it is very important for African American children to know African American history so they can see how we helped shape America. We are still separate and unequal, especially in the school system. When I read Jonathan Kozol's book, *Savage Inequalities*, it opened my eyes even wider. I had to do something to help educate our children. But you know what? It is up to the parents of our kids to teach them about the importance of education.

Anyway, enough rambling. It's a shame but I just got to work and I am ready to go home! It's Friday though and at least I will feel relieved when the bell rings at 3:15.

Monday, March 10, 2008

Why did I have to come in? I am sitting here having my breakfast as I type thinking if I could quit I probably would, BUT I CAN'T! I am just that frustrated. Is there any way out for me? Is it my destiny to be here? If it is, can't I change my destiny? Some would say the "kids need you there." I say "The kids need their parents to step up to the plate and be a parent, not a friend or buddy."

Every Sunday evening I get into this "funk" because I know I have to come to work. I was reading the local newspaper over the weekend how one school has a committee that addresses minority issues. Maybe we need something like that in my school... nah! It wouldn't do any good.

Again, I can remember how challenging it was during my first year as a guidance counselor. I, more or less, had to prove myself. Forget that I had over ten years experience in clinical counseling, I was a Black man in a school system where minority teachers, counselors, and other professionals come a dime a dozen. As a new guy on the block, you would expect them to share and help me get acclimated to the policies and procedures of the guidance department. There was no meeting, not even to introduce themselves to me as part of the team. I received very little help my first year.

I have been ridiculed, the focus of sly racist jokes, the whole nine yards, but what can I do? If I say something I would make more trouble for myself, so I just grin and bear it. Let's switch subjects now because my anger is building up like boiling lava reaching its peak in an agitated volcano.

Here is a good scenario of how kids fool their parents into believing they are totally innocent. A parent brought her son to school to complain that he was being bullied in the cafeteria. She informed me that he called her from the nurse's office crying. She also stated that he was afraid to come to school. He told her that he was shoved by another student and was hurt in the cafeteria and that no teachers were around to see the incident. First, this kid tells me everything that happens to him, why not this incident? Second, he is not afraid to come to school because he enjoys clowning in class and he can be a bully himself. He's playing you mom!

When she left I spoke with him privately. I told him that the next time I was going to tell his mother the truth and have her speak to the teachers about his behavior in class. I also informed him that I might call his mother to tell her how he passed a note around class and made a student cry because of what was written on it. He just stared at me. WAKE UP PARENTS! Please wake up.

Tuesday, March 11, 2008

Good morning! Today is starting out okay, other than my butt hurts from sitting on that little seat in my spin class. I had to get blood work done at

LabCorp this morning for my doctor's appointment on Friday. Yesterday was a quick "Monday" for me. Lunchtime was somewhat eventful. I had to tell a group of "tough guys" that they couldn't sit at the back table in the cafeteria.

Of course, they were angry and had to voice their opinion. "Mr. Wilson, oh my God, why do we have to move?" one student said while slowly getting up from his chair. Like a good counselor, my response was very nurturing and professional.

"Because I said so! I am the adult, you are the child, NOW GET UP!" I replied. They all got their lunches and moved with major attitudes. Did I care? No.

I believe society has embedded in the minds of children that they are on the same level as adults. Society has put into the minds of parents that you can be your child's friend or buddy. No. Not unless they are going to help you with the mortgage, rent, groceries, phone bill, gas bill, electric bill, and water bill! Children need to be children and stop trying to do adult things and make adult decisions.

I am out for now because I have to get ready for a meeting with my teachers. We basically go over the same students who are not doing well and acting out in class. What am I going to do about those students? Call the parents!

2:40 p.m.

It is now the end of the day. It was filled with student drama. A group of girls rushed into my office from lunch earlier and stated that they were going to get beaten by one girl. Okay. It was seven girls who were going to get beat up by one girl. They further stated that the girl was 'stalking' them though only during recess. Three words:

TOO MUCH TELEVISION.

I first explained to one of the girls involved in the recess episode that the other student was not 'stalking' them. Second, I asked her if one girl was going to beat up seven? After they had the girl in tears in recess, you would think that they would feel badly. Nope. Well, I have to talk with the students before I leave.

Wednesday, March 12, 2008

I am late getting to my journal entry this morning. I had a new student start today so I had to explain her schedule and take her on a tour of the school. On my way back to the office I was stopped by a teacher who asked me about a student who skipped her class. I told the teacher that I had him for the last ten minutes of eighth period (which means his counselor had him for thirty minutes.) The teacher stated that the student did not get permission to come to guidance.

I explained to the teacher that my students are not allowed in guidance without a pass. Basically, I was letting the teacher know that she needed to address his counselor on how the student came to the guidance office without a pass. If you have a grievance, go after the Black man. If you have a complaint, go after the Black man. If you want to commit a crime and get away with it, go after the BLACK MAN! That's how I feel.

It's just like the man who shot his pregnant wife, all he had to do was blame it on a Black man and he almost got away with it. The crazy lady who drove her kids into the river to drown, what did she do? She blamed it on the Black man and the police where kicking down doors in Boston looking for this man who supposedly carjacked her and drowned her kids.

I had dinner with a couple of friends of mine and I was telling them that we (Black men) are the most loved or the most hated. Example:

1. *2008's Most Loved Black Man in America (for right now) - Winner: Barack Obama*

2. *2008's Most Hated Black Man in America - Winner: (it's a three way tie) Michael Vick, any member of The Bloods street gang and any rapper who makes millions by exploiting Black women, writing senseless and meaningless lyrics, and consistently using the N-word.*

Are we ever going to get a break? I guess not in this lifetime. Well, I have to keep moving and doing what is right.

9:30 a.m.

A student just came into my office without a pass wanting to talk about drama that has been going on for the past three months. ALRIGHT ALREADY! LET IT GO! You know they are female students. My male students don't let things go on that long. "Mr. Wilson we need to talk about this situation. You need to call all of us down," she stated.

"Do you have a pass? How did you get out of class? Does your teacher know that you're down here? Does she know what's going on? What about your parents, do they know?" I kept asking her questions until she got frustrated and left. "I am going to bug you like you bug me!" I shouted with a big smile.

"I don't do that Mr. Wilson..." she said sincerely. Then I told her that I might call them down during the next period. "Are you sure? Are you going to call us down?" she said.

"Yeah, but if you ask me another question..." Before I could get it out she just rolled her eyes and smiled and returned to class.

You know, I am a very comforting and caring counselor. I address issues, both academic and social. That's where I transform into the caped crusader, Super Counselor - fighting the villains who spread ridiculous rumors and senseless middle school drama! Theme music please...

Thursday, March 13, 2008

Wow! I am hurting! I did the spin class again this morning. The class is challenging and very good for losing weight, but those seats are a killer! Anyway, the morning started off well. I came up with a good idea yesterday that I am going to implement for the sixth grade. I believe approximately 80-90% of issues for sixth graders here stem from bullying, rumors, or little arguments. Of that percentage, 50% derive from lunchtime and recess. Therefore, I set up a Counseling Table in the cafeteria where students can come to discuss rumors, issues with friends, or other little concerns.

Of course, any issue deemed confidential I have to discuss in private like family issues, etc. I started it yesterday and some students had legitimate issues. Others were being goofy until I informed them that I would call their parents to tell them about their behavior. I don't have much to discuss right now so I guess I will sign off... until something crazy happens and then I will be back. Well, I have kids to see and parents to call. Peace and blessings...

Friday, March 14, 2008

IT'S FRIDAY! And already the drama continues. Why are my young African American students so LOUD? Now let's get this straight, <u>not all</u> are loud, but the ones that are loud, ARE LOUD! One aspect I should point out is that some teachers take their loudness as being a behavior problem.

Let me interrupt my thought. I just had a student in my office, an African American male student, and he needed help with his tie. Lord knows that I want to teach all the male students how to tie a tie because if they want to be successful, one day they will probably have to wear one.

As I mentioned earlier, I was the eighth grade basketball coach this year and I required all the players to wear ties on game day. The effect it had on the students, staff, teachers, and administration was unbelievable. He came in asking me to help him. He had on a very nice suit, but I noticed his shirt was on backwards. "Why is your shirt on backwards?" I asked. Now, why do students tell a huge, long story that we really don't want to hear? Just get to the point and don't lie! I just looked at him and smiled and told him that if he wanted to wear his shirt inside out then that's fine with me. Anyway, I want to get back to my loud children.

For a lot of them, if there is yelling and screaming in the home, how do you think they are going to react in school? One time I had one of the students come to me and ask me for money. "MR. WILSON CAN I GET A DOLLAR?" she inquired almost shouting.

I said in a quiet whisper, "If you whisper, with a smidgen of politeness, I will give you two dollars."

She said "Shhhhhh, Mr. Wilson may I please have a dollar please?" First I told her not to say please twice in one sentence, then I gave her two dollars. She shouted, "THANK YOU! MR. WILSON, I'M JUST LOUD… THAT'S ME AND I GOTTA BE ME!" I just smiled and told her she didn't have to pay me back.

Well let me get to work, the children await. I have a student who took it upon himself to call a teacher 9:30 at night. He must have lost the little bit of mind he's got.

2:55 p.m.

It's the end of the day and in about five minutes the bell will ring for these students to go home. I felt invisible today. One thing sticks out in my mind that happened to me. A student was brought down from the nurse because another student hit him in the head with his binder. He came in with a big ice pack on his head. I spoke with the student and he gave the name of the other student so I looked him up on the computer to find out what class he was in for that period. I found out the class he was in and I contacted the front office to call him down.

Usually I speak to one of the secretaries but a teacher who had office duty answered instead. "Hello, can you call *Mikey* down for me he is in Room 22." He said okay. Two minutes later the teacher came down to see why I couldn't get up and call the student down myself. What? If it was one of the "other" counselors he would have called the student down without question.

I started to question myself. Is it a race thing? Is it a Black Male thing? Is it a male thing? Maybe it's all three? I think it is the first two, but hey, who am I?

Well it is 3:15 p.m.! That's our bell and I don't stay one second later! I try not to stay late unless I really have to. One counselor a couple of years ago made the comment that "...you're not a real counselor if you leave on time..." No, you're not a real counselor if you are not an advocate for **ALL** students. Since those remarks, I have been leaving at 3:15! I guess I am not a real guidance counselor.

Monday, March 17, 2008

Oh boy! I can't even get in the door and settle down. I had a student in my office crying this morning. I already knew the issue. MySpace!

Okay, I have a MySpace page to sell the music I produce. These children, however, use it as a vehicle to bully other kids, hook up with other kids, (and when I say hook up it doesn't mean getting together and going to Chuck E. Cheese), or other social things they can do. In this case, the student said that another student hacked into her Myspace page and changed her profile name. The student who supposedly did the hacking basically called her a 'lesbian'.

Of course the victim of this cyber bullying was very upset. She didn't want to go to homeroom, class, nor lunch in fear that she would be teased. Now, I instructed her that I would call her mother and let her know about our conversation and advise the mother to delete the Myspace page. The student looked at me as her tears rolled up her face and back into her eyes and said, "Do I have to delete my Myspace?" YES! And I put that weight on the parents!

If you know your child is being bullied on Myspace, IM, or any other computer vehicle, why let him or her continue to set themselves up? Either take the page offline or monitor your child's activities on the computer! You know, a lot of parents want the school to do something, but it happened IN THEIR HOUSE! Do they want me to come over and take the computer out of the wall and throw it away for them? All they have to do is BE A PARENT and tell their children that these are the rules of the house, follow them! There are no other options.

On a funny note, one of my students last week received a detention from a teacher for acting badly when a substitute was covering a class. He decided to tell the teacher that he is taking her to court! You should see my facial expression right now. The day of the detention he came to the Guidance Office looking for me. "Mr. Wilson, can you get me out of the detention? Please?"

I told him in a very stern voice, "I cannot talk to you without your lawyer present. Sorry!"

9:30 a.m.

Okay really quickly, I just received two e-mails from parents regarding their children. I don't know if this is a new thing with parents or what, but what is this about 'I don't want my child to know I contacted you about this'? Are you scared of your child? One parent got very upset with me because I told her son she called. Okay parents, let's remember, YOU ARE THE ADULT! WHAT YOU SAY GOES! If your child doesn't like it, tell them to get over it!

Don't have kids if you are going to be, as Bernie Mac puts it during his stand up in *The Kings of Comedy*, 'Punk *** Parents!' The one parent said to me on the phone, "Mr. Wilson I am upset that you told my son that I called you. I am really upset!" I apologized to her and informed her that the issued was resolved. I did tell her that I would transfer her to the principal's office if she wanted to make a formal complaint. She declined.

Now, what I felt like saying is this, "First, stop being a punk parent and be an adult. Your child had an issue and I resolved it, that's the important thing. If you are that worried that your child is going to say something to you then maybe you should work it out yourself!"

Tuesday, March 18, 2008

Slow morning. I ran my mile and did some weight training at the gym, now I am here. My morning preparation was interrupted by four female sixth graders who said it was too cold to go outside. If it is a nice day all of our students have to wait outside before the homeroom bell rings. Before I get into my morning excursion with my sixth graders, I was approached about helping out with eighth grade scheduling. Now, I have been saying for the past three years that I would like to learn the process of scheduling eighth graders for high school, but no one gave me any feedback. NOW, they want me to help out. Well, I am, because my ultimate goal is to become either a Vice Principal or Director of Guidance.

Well back to my morning drama with "four the hard way". I talked to them about the importance of doing well in school. One said she is failing gym. HOW DO YOU FAIL GYM? Quite frankly, she doesn't get changed. I told her to bring in five pairs of shorts and five t-shirts and to keep them in her locker, but she must take them home on the weekend to get washed. We didn't talk about much because I kept her focused on her academics. You know, when it comes to school work the children don't want to talk about much. Anyway, the homeroom bell rang so I told them to "Have a nice day, now GET OUT MY OFFICE!" They just laughed and left. I love the kids.

Wednesday, March 19, 2008

I woke up angry this morning. I didn't get a good night's sleep. I went to the gym angry. I just put my hoodie on and walked to the treadmill and didn't say a word to anyone. I ran my mile and did a quick shoulder workout. I tried to do my boxing workout but I couldn't. My anger drained me. Oops... I didn't say my prayers when I woke up. Excuse me for a second...

"Dear Jesus, please don't let these people get on my nerves at work. Please stop the students from coming to me for stupid reasons. Bless me and my wife, all my family, and my church family. Bless these kids in my school so they won't get on my nerves even though I know they will! Bless the sick and shut in. Bless all those I forgot to mention. In Jesus's name I pray, Amen"

Let me just say this, prayer is important. It keeps your sanity. It helps because you can do it at anytime, and it doesn't cost anything.

My ride home from the gym was intense. My thoughts of coming to work and being the only Black man here set me off. Since my fraternity brother left the school has there been any effort to hire any Black male professionals? Don't know. I don't even want to be bothered today. I don't have any conferences so I am going to stay in my office, make myself invisible.

Am I an angry Black man? I think I am just frustrated at times of what I have to go through just because I am a Black man. Harsh reality!

I had a student who wanted to speak to me. She filled out a guidance form. Let me explain our guidance forms. They were initiated to reduce the number of students coming to the guidance office. Remember I mentioned earlier how my first year the other guidance counselors in the guidance office complained that too many students were coming to my office? Well the guidance forms are a result of their complaints. On the form it asks the student's name, the date, his or her homeroom, which counselor they want to see, the type of problem (i.e. – scheduling, emergency, etc.) and what the problem is.

One student decided to put "I need to talk to you because I am being bullied by a teacher." HUH? I saw the student in the cafeteria and I asked her how she was being bullied by a teacher. She said that she is always yelling at her and telling her to stop talking.

"Are you serious?" I asked her. I told her that I think she is bullying the teacher. I said, "You won't sit down, your mouth is like the Energizer Bunny, you're constantly asking to go to the bathroom… you are causing the teacher pain. Maybe I should have your parents come in to talk with the teacher."

She quickly said, "Never mind I am okay."

"Listen," I said, "think and think hard before you fill out a guidance form. You hold two records in the sixth grade: one for the most forms filled out, and two for the most forms filled out for ridiculous reasons. Now go sit and eat your lunch before you and I have lunch together while we call your parents!"

8:25 a.m.

The vice principal came in to tell me that a parent is threatening to call the Board because we "are not doing what we said we will do." Okay, I forgot ONE TIME to give the student a progress report and mom wants to call the Board of Education. This is the same mother who says her son is being bullied every day. Honestly, he instigates with other kids but can't take it when they retaliate. Mom doesn't want to hear the whole story, but you know what? When he gets older, she is going to be in for it. I am going to call her right now and tell her that the teachers want to meet with her. I bet any amount of money she can't meet with the teachers. Hold on...

Well I would lose my money, she's coming in next week. The question is, what good will it do? We shall see.

12:00 p.m.

Sometimes lunch duty is challenging, especially for my mental sanity! The kids just follow me around for no reason. They don't want anything! I actually hid behind the vending machine today and the principal walked in. "Are you hiding Mr. Wilson?" he asked with a surprised look on his face.

"YES!" I replied with confidence. To give you an example of what I am talking about, I had a female student come up to me with an issue.

"Mr. Wilson I have an issue. It's real important."

Well, I said to myself, *she is a good student and she hardly has any issues except for one where she was crying because she broke up with a boy after knowing him for ONE DAY!* "What's wrong?" I replied.

16

"Well can you talk to the kitchen workers because the bread for my hoagie was hard?" She almost made me quit! I told her to see if they would give her bread. She didn't want to go ask. So I went into the kitchen to see if I could get her another roll. I put on the charm and they gave me another roll. "Mr. Wilson this looks hard too," she said. *TAKE THE ROLL!* I said in my mind. I told her that all the bread was hard because they left it sitting out too long and the aroma from other students' breath who didn't gargle made it even harder. "Okay Mr. Wilson, thanks!" Wow, what a story I gave her!

Another student started following me playing the "air" guitar. Three more students followed me to talk about the same issue they have been talking about for over a month now. One student doesn't know why she followed me, she just followed me. One student stood in front of me to say "Hi," then after I said "hi" back she just stares at me.

"Is there something I can help you with?" I asked being slightly frustrated. She shook her head "no," but still continued to stand there. FOR WHAT? GO SIT DOWN! NOW! PLEASE?

One student followed me and talked by screaming at the top of her lungs. "MR. WILSON… MR. WILSON… MR. WILSON!" she yelled.

"Could you please turn down your speakers? What do you want?" I asked.

"NOTHING!" as she giggled and trotted away. I am going to produce a new Horror film entitled: *CHILDREN OF THE CORNey: CURSE OF THE MIDDLE SCHOOL KIDS DURING LUNCH TIME!*

Do I deserve this? Why me? Part of the reason that I believe students latch on to me is that they have NEVER seen a Black man up close, or they have never developed a relationship with a Black man who is caring and nice. It's a shame how we are only associated with gangs, violence, rap stars, and anything negative, especially our youth. It is even more disheartening when guidance counselors make judgments like that and never do anything to address the problem. But guess what? SURPRISE! All Black men are not like that. In fact I believe that there are more upstanding brothers with character and diligence than there are in prison. We have been through the toughest situations. We have handled the worst. We can get along with anyone. We can relate to anyone, however, everyone cannot relate to us.

Thursday, March 20, 2008

Last day before spring break… THANK GOD! I took the spinning class at the gym this morning. Those spinning bike seats aren't made for brothas! My behind still hurts. I have two parent conferences today and hopefully it will make the day go by faster. I am ready for Spring break!

I need a break from this place. My invisibility is getting the best of me. I try and socialize but I feel like I don't fit in. I don't have anything to talk about. Many times I just find myself standing there just smiling. I have to smile to make myself look passive and not aggressive. You know how people start treating Black men if we look and act a certain way. Oh, and don't let us start talking about injustice especially regarding race.

During certain conversations, I turn on my 'super powers' and make myself invisible. I constantly keep myself busy to keep my mind focused while my ears tune out the distractions around me. God forbid if Black staff had a jolly old time.

We had a special celebration for our Black History Month program yesterday. It brought a smile to my face to see Black students getting along with each other without bickering, fighting, or any type of drama. Our principal bought them pizza to congratulate them on a successful program. They devoured it. One student actually tried to take a box! WHY? I told her to put the box back and of course she refused. So I went up to her and began to talk very quietly (I speak with our Black students in a soft voice because many of them hear screaming and hollering at home all the time). I said, "*Jameera* why do you have an entire box of pizza to yourself? You know our history, Black history, is about sharing with others. We helped each other along the way that's how we got through slavery, Jim Crow, the Civil Rights movement, and any struggle that came our way."

She replied, "I understand that Mr. Wilson, but this ain't slavery or Civil Rights. We in the cafeteria and I'm hungry so this Black girl gonna help herself to some pizza. Is that alright with you Mr. Wilson?"

I looked at her and laughed and said to her, "Do your people a favor and give me a slice!" She looked at me and laughed and gave me the smallest slice in the pie. My final words to her before I went to go bother some other students were, "Remember, go to college and not just for the parties!"

She started dancing with the pizza box in her hand and replied, "Mr. Wilson why else am I going to college… gotta get it on!" Then about six other students came and joined her in a quick dance with melodic hip hop beats coming from the mouths.

I just had a parent come in for my first conference. Parents usually have two facial expressions when they see me: one, the reaction is shock. They can't believe their child has a Black male guidance counselor! Oh my God! The second is an element of relief. I mainly see that from Black parents. It's almost a sigh of relief. The parent sitting out there now, who is twenty-five minutes early, had the first reaction. I just look at them, smile, greet them pleasantly and get straight to business.

Monday, March 31, 2008

Spring Break is over! Back to school to complete the LAST HAUL! I was in the gym this morning telling another staff member that I didn't want to come back to work. I was telling him how I don't feel comfortable and I am always on edge being the only Black man besides the custodian in the building. His remarks put everything in perspective for me. "You know some people don't have jobs. So be thankful you got somewhere to go…" Yup! I am thankful for all the blessings God has given me and continues to give me. But I can't help the way I feel.

These are the last two and a half months of school and I can't wait! I just had two students come to my office because they didn't want to wait outside. It was one student's birthday and she was very happy about that. I asked the students what they did for Spring Break. Most didn't do anything fun or exciting, "Mr. Wilson I just hung out and talked to my friends on Myspace..."

I believe one of the problems for most students is their inactivity in positive extracurricular activities. I believe it also contributes to the obesity epidemic among teens. I remember growing up how we were ALWAYS outside! If it rained, we were waiting by the window for it to clear up! Our generation remained active. Of course, back then all we had was Atari for video games. I had *Asteroids* and *Pitfall*. Television ended at a certain time.

Today, kids can live in their room for hours. That's why for a punishment parents should make kids go outside instead of going to their rooms. Parents should make kids eat a healthy meal instead of taking a meal away for a punishment. Our children are exposed to so much too soon.

The amount of sex and violence these children are exposed to is alarming. It seems as though America cannot sell anything without associating it with sex or violence. When children see this every day, I feel it becomes a part of their lives and their way of thinking. From television to music being played on their iPods, this decadent way of life, of sex, drugs, and violence, is being buried in their subconscious minds. Well enough preaching, I have to get to work. I have three parents to call, a parent/teacher conference, and students to see before the day is over.

2:35 p.m.

Twenty-five minutes until the students leave. I made it through! Again, I felt invisible today so I just stayed in my office and caught up on some paperwork. I overheard one staff member come in and talk about how they spent Spring Break in a town I have never heard of before.

I remember my dad took us to Nebraska. We went to a restaurant and I looked around. I said, "Dad, I don't see any Black people..."

He quietly said, "That's okay, we're here…" I told him I didn't want to be there and refused to eat. I still find myself going into restaurants looking for other African Americans. Just a little childhood flashback.

I have ten minutes until the bell rings. Let me just say some issues are not black and white, they are who has money and who is broke! The rich and the poor, the "haves" and the "have nots." Anyway, tomorrow will be a different day.

Tuesday, April 1, 2008

April Fool's day! I should have called out and said "Ya'll thought I was coming in… APRIL FOOL!" The gym was a killer this morning, but I got through it. I was talking to my frat brother in the gym about how I want to work in an urban district with more minority youth. I asked him if he was comfortable where he is teaching. He said he is because he likes the environment. Of course there is a much better ratio of Black teachers to White teachers and the majority of the student population is Black. Oh well, thank God I have a job.

I just looked on my desk and saw an instant message that was printed out and given to me of two students going back and forth with threatening and obscene messages. Cyber-bullying is a big problem at my school and nationally, especially text messaging and on Myspace. Why don't parents monitor this more? I don't know. Kids are TOO spoiled these days. Parents set some boundaries and don't spare the rod! Well I don't want to start rambling on.

11:30 a.m.

Lunch duty was horrible. It was raining and we couldn't go outside. At one point I had five students following me around the cafeteria. What did they want? NOT A THING! I had one little boy come to me and say, "Mr. Wilson I have issues." I looked up to the ceiling out of frustration because he says he has issues every day and the only issue is that he won't sit down and eat lunch.

"What happened?" I replied.

"This kid in my neighborhood…" he began to explain.

"STOP!" I said. "Do you see your house in this cafeteria because if you don't then this IS NOT your neighborhood! THIS IS SCHOOL!" He just turned and bopped away laughing. I think they work my nerves on purpose.

Ms. "I Am Going 2 Scream at the Top of My Lungs" came up to me again. "MR. WILSON, MR. WILSON, MR. WILSON I HAVE AN ISSUE!"

I said, "I do too! The fact that you can't whisper is a problem!"

Suddenly she whispered, and then shouted, "Mr. Wilson you know… YOU'RE RIGHT I CAN'T WHISPER!" Where do they come from? Then I had two gentlemen come to me because they spilled chocolate milk on each other.

The last student who approached me asked if she could get her schedule changed. I wanted to shout, "IT'S THE END OF THE THIRD MARKING PERIOD!" However, my answer was short and sweet… "NO."

Wednesday, April 2, 2008

(Singing in tune)

> *It's a beautiful day in this neighborhood,*
> *A beautiful day for a neighbor.*
> *Would you be mine?*
> *Could you be mine?*

> *It's a neighborly day in this beauty wood,*
> *A neighborly day for a beauty.*
> *Would you be mine?*
> *Could you be mine?*

I've always wanted to have a neighbor just like you.
I've always wanted to live in a neighborhood with you.

So, let's make the most of this beautiful day.
Since we're together we might as well say:
Would you be mine?
Could you be mine?
Won't you be my neighbor?
Won't you please,
Won't you please?
Please won't you be my neighbor?

That is the opening song to *Mr. Roger's Neighborhood*. I grew up on that show. I am in a good mood and it's "hump" day (Wednesday). I was doing just fine until I had a SWARM of students at my door. They didn't want anything! You know, everyday, I thank God I don't have kids. I tell people I have three hundred of them every school year!

Anyway, I grew up on *Mr. Rogers' Neighborhood*, as well as *Sesame Street* and the *Electric Company*. Those television shows taught me a lot. Television, in my opinion, when I was growing up, seemed more educational. In between cartoons on channel six there was "Conjunction junction, what's your function?" and "I am only a Bill!" Now if you don't know what I am talking about I am probably older than you or you didn't watch cartoons on Saturday mornings during 1975-1983. Also, television went off at 11:00 or 11:30 p.m. The American flag would wave and the "Star Spangled Banner" would play. After the song was over all you saw was static! Every station! Now, kids can stay up all night! Cartoons are much, much more violent! Children do not go outside anymore. Even fighting is different. Yes, let's talk about it.

Back in the day it was a fair fight and when it was over, it was OVER! Whoever won, won and that was it. Nowadays, it's a vendetta! Weapons are involved! Families are involved! Revenge is involved! It can be ongoing for days, months, and even years! What a shame! What happened to our children, our generation?

The influx of gangs is a major problem, especially in the Black community. The absence of parents, family structure, and love for family, (both immediate and extended) is key in the breakdown of our children not succeeding, especially in the Black community. Why am I called to work with youth? (Notice I said 'called'). I believe God has chosen me to work with young people. I have developed a tolerance level when it comes to youth. I enjoy working with youth, especially youth in the Black community. Fathers and father figures have disappeared. Obsolete… For a young black male to have a father is like me trying to do Phase I of the South Beach diet. Rare! (I'm never doing Phase I of South Beach again!) I have to do something about this epidemic.

9:00 a.m.

I just had a twelve-year old boy in my office saying he didn't want to go to class. As a counselor, I spoke with him and eventually got him to stop crying and go back to class. What I really wanted to say was *"Take your big behind to class! You're too big for this! You're the biggest sixth grader in the building and you act like you're in kindergarten! Get out of my office and grow up!"* But I can't because I am a professional and I can't respond like that as a counselor. I brought him in and began to speak with him about what was bothering him. Eventually, he felt better and I walked him to his class.

Quite frankly, I believe the behaviors of some students are a lack of love, prayer, and beatin's! You have to have all three! Those three things kept me out of jail, off the streets, and in school. Most importantly, we have to look at the family structure and where the breakdown occurred and try and alleviate the problem before it starts to get out of control. Love, prayer, and discipline kept me out of jail, off the streets, and in school. I had a wonderful relationship with my parents. I was respectful to my parents (something that is missing today). I appreciate all the love my parents gave me growing up. They made me who I am today.

2:15 p.m.

I just had a student who needed help studying his definitions. He came in with a huge smile on his face (I think he just wanted to get out of class but he had a pass.) I started going over...

OH NO! One of my favorite but nerve wracking students just came in! She works my nerves so badly! She doesn't listen! I told her to leave my office and she is still sitting there. She is actually talking to me while I am typing. She knows I am not listening but she continues to talk. About what? I don't know because I am trying to do some work.

Now you are probably asking "What kind of guidance counselor are you?" First, my priority is sixth graders and this student is in eighth grade. Wait, she just asked me if I was listening to her. I said "No!", but she is continuing to talk. Why? She is telling me how she cussed her grandmother out. Okay, get your own house and food then! Why is she still talking? Guess what, one of her friends came in. Oh Lord! Let me just pay attention to them so they can get out more quickly.

Thursday, April 3, 2008

Yesterday was "Hug Mr. Wilson Day." No matter what I tell the students they still try and hug me. I am NOT trying to catch a case! I tell them over and over "You can't hug me it's against the law! Hug your parents and tell them you love them! Don't hug me please, or I will get fired!" I know you don't want to hear it but I am going to say it anyway. I don't want to hug these germy, never wash my hands, coughing and sneezing all over the place kids! Now, all of the students are not nasty, but many of them do not take care of themselves.

I especially don't want to be hugged by female students. In today's society, when you have so many perverse individuals, plus the way the media portrays Black men in a negative light, I don't want them touching me. I even keep my door slightly open with female students. If they happen to come in to talk and shut the door behind them, I quietly say, "Sorry I have to open the door a little because it gets stuffy and uncomfortable." As much as I say to them stop hugging, poking, hitting me to get my attention they act as if they are totally deaf!

Why don't they listen? Why can't they understand? Parents teach your children to listen. In addition, be good listeners also but don't believe everything kids tell you without getting all the facts. I hate it when parents come in angry because their child LIED to them. I want to tell them that they are worse than the kids!

We had a staff meeting yesterday on how to use a computer on a cart. Wow! Yet again I just chose to sit in the back and work by myself. I took inventory; there were only three of us this time. We are diminishing fast. I went to go get a laptop from the computer guy and he made a joke as if I didn't work here. I showed him my badge and gave him an angry look. I just took the computer and went in the café. I guess the Lord didn't bless me with quick-witted responses because he knew that I may be in trouble all my life.

I just feel people with quick responses to people's senseless comments are left alone. I have one parent who is like that and everyone at the school just dreads seeing her. I like it. I get along with her well. She went off on me one time and I just sat and looked at her and said, "We are family. What can I do to help? I am not against you, I am with you. There's a certain way I have to act and present myself around here or some staff will give me a hard way to go and I can possibly lose my job." She has never gone off on me since. Anyway, yes during the staff meeting I had an invisible moment but I didn't care. I am just ready for school to end.

10:10 a.m.

Okay, I just got off the phone with one of my colleagues. One of my associates, (a person I know but who is not a close friend), just got busted for drugs! Why do brothers do this to themselves? His son attends middle school and it is a shame that the cycle is continuing to turn. He came from a good family, however, my boy made the wrong decision.

Wow! I just found out that one of my students was committed to an intensive inpatient program. The student was suicidal according to the guardian. I tried to call her case worker from DYFS but of course, no answer. I tried to talk with the student on many occasions. She opened up in our counseling sessions, however, she hated our school and her living situation. I felt sorry for her. The student had a history of cutting. I emphasized to her and her family to seek professional help.

1:35 p.m.

I just came back from seeing a group of kids on a field trip! The kids were following me around singing! They sounded like wounded geese. Horrible! From the "Sponge Bob" song to raps by Soldja Boy, (I don't know how he spells it)! I couldn't walk around to all the students because the group kept following me. Then I had a kid who wanted to take his medicine without water. "Mr. Wilson, I don't need no water," he said bouncing all over the place.

"Well you need to start paying attention in Language class so you can stop using double negatives in a sentence," I replied. "And yes you do need to drink water to take your meds." He had the attention span of a newborn puppy being released outdoors for the first time! I was talking to one teacher out there and we both agreed that we are medicating children too much. I am sure that in some households back in the day, a bottle of cough syrup and a good spanking cured everything! If your feet hurt the solution was "Boy either you get me the cough syrup or stop runnin' around this house!"

Oh yeah, before I forget, I spoke to my wife as I was driving and she told me how frustrated she was at a parent. She is a high school guidance counselor. The parent was angry because her daughter was removed from a special program. Okay, in a nutshell, the student was drunk in a public place and got arrested. Oh yeah, the student was underage. Okay parent, you're going off on my wife but don't care if your child has a career in public drunkenness? Your child might not graduate because they are skipping school to go to the liquor store to get some beer or liquor that someone else had to buy. GET YA HEAD IN THE RIGHT PLACE LADY! Whenever you see a kid that has issues, remember, the apple does not fall far from the tree. *Keep your head up baby and don't worry about that parent. Know that I love you…* I'm out… got work to do.

Friday, April 4, 2008

IT'S FRIDAY! I made it through the week. Yes! I have a good weekend planned! I cannot wait until 3 p.m.! Look at me, I just got here and already I am ready to leave.

Yesterday I saw some students I had in sixth grade and now they are in high school. They have grown so much. I asked them if they are ready for the real world, they said "No we are still having fun." I just smiled. I have to speak with a student this morning - Wait my phone is ringing.

I just got a phone call from my godsister, my godfather passed. He was battling cancer for a long time. He was a pastor, a father, a leader; he was an upstanding Black man. He supported his family and was a pillar of the community. He helped me get a summer job at PSE&G when I was in college. We used to have long talks about life and family. God rest his soul. Well, God knows what is best.

I let my principal know and he said whatever I needed to do, just do it. I don't have any time left or anything, but he worked it out for me. I have to say, I enjoy working for my administration. They are fair. My principal is good! That's a blessing! He is a good man! I like the teachers I work with and I get along with them well because they know my focus is on the students.

Getting back to the student I was talking about earlier. He called a teacher a racist and received a green slip, (what teachers fill out for disciplinary action on a student), for it. I am going to speak to him about his behavior in class and his accusation.

Many of our Black students use that term loosely and they tend to throw it around at white teachers. I ask students who make these accusations, one, have they ever treated you unfairly because of the color of your skin? "No." Have they called you the N-word to your face? "No." Have they proven to you to be racially biased when class projects are given or excluded you from field trips because you were Black? "No." Were you acting up in class while the teacher was trying to teach? "Mr. Wilson all I did…" STOP! Nine times out of ten, the student was wrong and when called out on it they got in trouble and now the teacher is a racist. Then I begin to ask students questions about Slavery, Jim Crow laws, the Civil Rights Movement. They look at me like I have two heads and a booger hanging out my nose! I tell them to go educate themselves on African American history and obey the rules of the classroom.

One time I had a white student say that a white teacher was being racist towards her. I looked at her and told her to "Get Out!" She had four F's out of five classes. I told her that she was being racist towards me because she kept coming down to the Guidance Office for stupid reasons. She just smiled and trotted out of my office.

I have to get to work.

Monday, April 7, 2008

It's Monday morning and yes, I don't feel like being here. My weekend was too short and too busy. Yesterday, after I came home from church, I just slept all day. As soon as I walked in the door, after heating up my breakfast, I had a parent and a student waiting. First, I believe it should be an official rule that parents MUST call and make an appointment. You can't just walk into a doctor or lawyer's office and expect to be seen right away; you have to make an appointment. I believe the school should be the same way especially if you have a lot of students.

I didn't mind seeing this parent, she was very concerned about her son. I had to send her a warning letter regarding her son being retained. However, they were basically homeless for the entire second marking period. I spoke with our principal about it and the student probably won't stay back. It was very interesting that the mother wanted her son to get extra work for him to catch up academically.

The other student that came into the office wanted to talk about the same crap we resolved on Friday. "Mr. Wilson, *Christy* wants to fight me," she said in a concerned voice.

"Did she approach you? Did she jump in your face? What did she say?" I replied.

"She didn't say anything, *Betty* told me and..."

"STOP!" I said in a stern voice. "So basically you're going to get five days suspension because of what someone else said?" She just stared at me. So I stared back at her. Her eyes got bigger, and then my eyes got bigger.

"Mr. Wilson, I'm going to get suspended?" she said in a quivery voice.

"If you fight you will." I told her that I will meet with her, *Betty*, and *Christy* to resolve this whole issue.

AHHHHH! I just heard the morning announcements and our staff meeting is postponed. Thank you Jesus! I want to go home. Some people are just lucky.

I wish I could do music full time but I can't. It gets frustrating sometimes not being able to do what you REALLY want to do. Oh well, life goes on.

Anyway, it is back to work. I have a parent coming in whose son gets on everyone's nerves but she thinks he is being bullied. Her eyes are about to be opened wide. She is in for a big surprise. She will probably go into denial that her son instigates with other students. Oh well, at least she is going to realize the truth.

11:30 a.m.

Guess what? You guessed it. Just came back from lunch duty. This lunch duty was comical. First I went back and sat on the radiator next to my "Counseling Table" and the loud student I mentioned earlier in the book bounced by. She just waved. I shouted, "*LeAnn* it's good to see you and not hear you!"

She turned around and said in a loud voice, "WHAT?" I just closed my eyes and began to imagine I was in Jamaica. Then three girls came up to me for no reason. The first student I made a special handshake with and she wants to do it everyday! Oh my goodness! Then "*Mr. I Am Going to Take My Teacher to Court*" stuck his middle finger up at a student so I made him sit by me in lunch. "Mr. Wilson, why do I have to sit back here with you?," he said out of frustration.

"Why do you have to come to school?" I replied.

"Because I have to."

"Exactly!"

He just blew his breath out of frustration. After feeling his breath scrape the tips of my nose hairs, I told him, "I suggest you don't even ask a question in class unless you chew a Tic Tac!" He looked at me and started laughing. I smiled at him and told him how he likes when I give him attention. He just looked at me over the top of his glasses.

He always does that. He never looks through his glasses, only over top of them. I asked him one time when he was in my office crying because he was sent out of class, "Why do you wear glasses? You never look through them." He tried not to laugh because he wanted me to believe he was crying. I said, "You know why you wanna laugh? BECAUSE YOU KNOW I'M RIGHT!" He started laughing through his glasses.

Anyway, getting back to the cafeteria, I had a young man bring a bag of popcorn out for recess. Okay, the rule is NO FOOD OUTSIDE! I called him over to me in the middle of the basketball court. "Uhh, *Joseph* why do you have a bag of popcorn out here?" I asked.

"What Mr. Wilson? I don't have any popcorn," he replied with a smirk on his face.

I took the bag from him after he refused to give it up and mashed the bag so that all the popcorn would crumble. I then said, "Take your pick the puddle or the garbage can." He looked at me as to say "I don't care!" So I threw it in the garbage can and informed him that he cannot play basketball for two weeks for breaking the rules.

One girl decided to come up to me and tell me that she has a seventh grade boyfriend. She said it with pride and a huge grin on her face. So I said as she was bouncing up and down, "I am sooo happy for you! Now let's go tell your dad the good news!" Her smile went to a frown!

One thing I have concluded as a sixth grade guidance counselor: recess is always full of dramatic events.

Tuesday, April 8, 2008

It's Tuesday and I am tired. Half of the sixth grade went on an overnight trip. I am doing some workshops for the students who didn't go on the trip, it should be fun. It is getting closer to the end of the year. I was actually telling one of our counselor's that the last two weeks of school seem like the longest part of the school year. We are getting out on the twentieth of June, (about two and a half months), then it's summer break.

Well I don't have much to write - oh wait, the vice principal did approach me yesterday towards the end of school to talk about a student. We are both hesitant to contact mom because the woman can have a very negative disposition about her sometimes. I get along with her fine, we have gotten into it before; however, I just looked at her and started thinking about my music while she was rambling. I told my Vice Principal to have the student work in my office all day.

I did ask if his counselor spoke with him about his behavior and why he is getting green slips. His counselor didn't. Okay, question... What are we as guidance counselors here for? Just to talk to certain students? I don't know.

We shouldn't give up on students no matter how "HARD HEADED" they are. That's why I am glad I worked in social services for twelve years before I came here. In my opinion, you don't need a lot of teaching experience to be a counselor. You need to be knowledgeable of student issues and student resources, especially those in the community. By me keeping this young man in my office it just grants me an opportunity to work with another young Black male student, and trust me, he's going to work.

10:00 a.m.

I have the student in my office and I gave him plenty to read. Most of it is on African American History. He is actually studying for a quiz I am going to give him on African American History. I informed him that in order to get his cell phone back he must pass with at least a seventy percent. "Aww Mr. Wilson! I paid fifty dollars for that cell phone with my own money! It's not fair," he said with a frustrated voice.

"Get over it and keep studying," I replied. I believe that African American History should be integrated into our curriculums. It may give some Black students, especially male students, a sense of pride in education if they knew how hard we fought. Hold on, I just asked my student if he would do better and act better if there was an African American History course in school. "Hey *Al* if there was a Black history course here that taught about how hard we fought for you to get an education, would you do better in school and stop getting into trouble?" I asked.

"Yeah Mr. Wilson, of course," he affirmed.

"Why do you consistently lie to me?" I replied. That boy is off the chain and it will take more than a history course to make him act right. He just lied to me with a straight face. He's a good boy though, just too busy. Now he is asking for the quiz. He studied for a good two minutes. Wow!

11:30 a.m.

I just came from lunch duty and I have a big problem. I have a group of students, (girls of course), who don't think there is anything wrong with saying the N-word. I am sorry, but my female students cause more drama and actually fight more than the boys! Two of the girls have this handshake where at the end they say 'My Niggaz!' Now one of the girls was not Black and I was looking at her as if to say "You have no right to say that word and if you do…" I need all the rappers and youth to stop using the N-word. I told the girls to stop using that word especially in front of me. I don't like it!

OH NO! Here comes an eighth grade student who works my nerves. She doesn't stop talking! I just told this student to get out, but she didn't listen because she said she has a problem, so you know I had to make myself available. You have to love the children. "Mr. Wilson I got a problem," she shouts.

"Go talk to your counselor," I told her as I turned around to finish typing. And guess what? You guessed it. She kept right on talking about absolutely NOTHING! I wish you could listen through this book you would probably throw it away! Oh my God, she just keeps going. I even closed my eyes and said a quick prayer.

"Mr. Wilson, you listening to me? 'Cause if you're not I'm leaving!" she exclaimed.

"No, I'm not listening. Not a single word. I am officially deaf." Of course she laughed and continued to talk. HELP!

Thursday, April 10, 2008

The principal and I went on a trip yesterday to visit our students who are on an overnight trip. I always like the drive up and back because we get to talk and bond about a lot of things. I always ask him what I can do to improve issues of students at my middle school. We always talk about ideas and goals. We had a good ride up. When we arrived the students were happy to see the both of us. Of course I had to make my rounds around the breakfast table. I also spoke with some of the teachers to see who was acting up, who was homesick, if there were any incidents that happened in the first couple of days. Luckily, there were only a few. It was nice for once to not have any major issues come my way. Then it happened.

I went to go visit one of the activities with the principal where the students climb into a net that is hung between four trees and they have to climb in and flip out with the assistance of the activity leader. One student decided that he wanted to climb in; however, we noticed he wouldn't flip out. All the students climbed in and flipped out. Suddenly he started to cry.

He didn't want to flip out. Well, we said fine we can help you out. He shook his head. We told the other students to go to the next activity while we got the student down. It took us half an hour to get him down. I reached in and grabbed him out, holding him in my arms like a baby so that he wouldn't fall. He told us that he was afraid of heights. *Did you know that before you climbed in? Did you see how high the net was? Why did you climb in?* Those were the questions running through my mind. The principal, the trip director, a supervisor, and myself were there trying to talk with him and he just wouldn't respond.

Wait! I just had a student come into my office. I saw him one day with a jean chain connected to his wallet. "I like that 'D' where did you get it?" I asked.

"I got it from Kmart," he replied.

"Hey the next time you go pick me up one. Now don't do the five finger lift off (five finger lift off = stealing), but get me one," I said while giving him a pound, (you know that's a hand shake that brothers incorporated a while ago).

He said "Okay."

"Look I am just playing. Use your hard earned money for your little girlfriend or better yet YOUR MOTHER!"

Well, his case manager walked into my office and said "*Samuel* would like to speak with you."

He came in and pulled out the jean chain with the wallet and said with a deep quiet voice, "Here you go Mr. Wilson." My eyes were opened wide because I thought he was in trouble even though I am not his counselor.

"*Samuel* I was just playing! You didn't have to buy me that man!" I stood up and gave him, what I call a "brother2brother" hug. That's when you shake hands while the opposite arm wraps around the other brother's torso which means "I want to give you a hug without being feminine." That just made my day. I am going to end this journal entry on a positive note. I have taken this young man to lunch and dinner just to speak with him about his behavior and just that little token of him giving me a jean chain wallet just confirmed that I can't and I won't give up on our young Black males NO MATTER WHAT THE COST! I challenge all the professional brothers to give a young Black male a "brother2brother" hug!

Sunday, April 13, 2008

It's Sunday evening and yes I am mentally preparing myself for work tomorrow. I know, some of you may say "Why don't you just relax and worry about work tomorrow?" Well, I can't. I can't wait until the end of the school year. That is our last day of school.

I have to tell you, I haven't written in my journal in a while and so much has happened but there is one thing I have to mention to you. I did a workshop for my sixth graders who did not go on the overnight trip and I have come to two conclusions: one, either our kids are plain brainless; or two, there is no, I mean NO education going on at home! Some of you are saying right now that our kids are just plain stupid, but I disagree. We are missing the education and discipline at home. Let me give you some examples of how our kids "missed the boat."

"Missed the boat" is an expression I used to describe people who don't use common sense, or the answer is right in front of them and they still get it wrong. I started the workshop with a fun activity, just to get them loose. It was a common sense quiz with questions like "How many curves are in a standard paper clip?" Three right? Yes, there are three. I asked the question, "In which hand is the Statue of Liberty holding the torch?"

"Ooo Ooo Ooo!" one student shouted. "Mr. Wilson it depends on where you are standing. It could be the left or the right." Huh? She "missed the boat" and it's sailing right in front of her. It doesn't matter where you stand sweetheart, it's still in her RIGHT HAND!

Wait, don't laugh too hard yet, that's not at the top of the "I Think I'm Mentally Challenged" charts. The teacher in the workshop with me asked the class, "In what year did Christopher Columbus discover America?" You know what one girl said? Ready? 1962! That's the doggone Civil Rights Movement! Oh my goodness. Wait I am not finished.

I asked the class "How many states are in the United States of America?"

"Mr. Wilson there are 23 states!" one girl said firmly. Oh… my… God! We are in trouble. If Whitney Houston really meant what she said when she sang the song "I believe the children are the future…" no wonder she was interviewed by Barbara Walters and asked for receipts for crack purchases on national television. Just say "no" to drugs and being stupid! I told them there were fifty and I needed them to list at least twenty-five.

One girl asked the teacher in a quiet voice, "Ms. Teacher, is Africa a state?" My Jesus! One student listed Canada! What is going on? Africa! Canada? Parents please turn off the television, take the cell phone, take the iPod, just take everything and make them READ. They should have known this stuff by the third grade! Africa a state? Our young generation needs help! They thought the green light was on the top of the traffic light, but they can't wait to drive! Let's take a break from the LAND OF THE FREEminded, HOME OF THE BRAVEly dim-witted and they are proud of it! I believe that they think it is cool not knowing important information.

Oh well… I was talking with my sister in church and I was telling her how mentally draining it is to be the only African American male at work without anyone to talk to about my issues, concerns, and feelings. She said that I should start an organization of Black male guidance counselors or Black men in education. You know what, I am going to try. Well let me get a nap because my wife and my dog are asleep and I am wide awake.

Monday, April 14, 2008

It's finally here. Today is the first day of the FOURTH MARKING PERIOD! I am so happy that I only have approximately two months left of school. I feel good today. I am in good spirits.

Now let's talk about what happened with my sixth graders during the overnight trip. One minute in the door and I got a report about Friday. Overall, the sixth graders were good. Nevertheless, I got a report about two sixth graders getting into a "scuffle" the last day of the overnight trip.

The main factor of the scuffle was one student called the other student the N-word. Here we go. I have to deal with this issue again. Now in your mind you are thinking another Black child being called the N-Word, right? Wrong! Both students were white. Yes, a white student called another white student a "n****r." Wow! This tells me that this word is used too loosely in society and in the home. It needs to be banned and, especially students, need to see some serious consequences when using the word. I believe it's worse than profanity because, for me, it's personal.

Anyway, I walked down to the student's homeroom to speak with him. He knew I was upset because usually he would try to give me a "brother2brother" hug and say "What's good Mr. Wilson?" He did not say a word.

I sat him down and said "*Rich* do you know why I brought you down here?"

"Yes," he replied with a soft voice while looking over the top of his glasses as to give me the "I'm soo sorry, puppy eyes." IT DID NOT WORK!

I said, "I heard you got into a little scuffle with *Nate* and called him the N-word."

"Yes," he replied.

"First, let's handle the scuffle then let's talk about the N-word. How did it start?" I asked him.

"Well *Nate* and another student started playing with my hat and I got tired of it."

"Did you tell a teacher?" I asked.

"I told my counselor but he didn't do anything. So I got mad."

"Is that when you called him the N-word?"

"Yes," he replied trying to use the puppy dog eyes again.

"First, I am going to let the vice principal know that these students were taking your hat and the counselor did not do anything. Second, let's talk about the name you called them. You know that word offends me right?"

"Yes…"

"That word was invented to dehumanize African Americans. Even though today you may hear it in some music it is still meant to degrade Black people. I don't like it when Black students use the word. Please let this be the last time you use that word!"

"Mr. Wilson I'm sorry."

"No problem. But you can make it up to me." I said.

"How?" he responded as his body perked up and his eyes brightened.

"By making honor roll and not giving the teachers a hard time this marking period." His shoulders sunk as he sucked his teeth and rolled his eyes up to the air. I just smiled and said, "That's what school is all about!"

On a good note, one sixth grade student who has had difficulty for most of the year here actually received kudos from his teachers and counselors during the overnight trip. He actually wants to be a biologist. I am going to talk with him about his new aspirations and encourage him to pursue his goals. You know what, I am going to end it here on a good note! Peace and love…

12:15 p.m.

I had a meeting earlier in the day about a program that we are implementing in our school. I truly believe that some people just take a Black man's opinion for a grain of salt. No matter how much experience I have or how much I know, my opinion doesn't matter. I have a strategy when I attend planning meetings. First I sit and listen, especially to other staff's grandioso ideas. Then I take an assessment of what to say making sure I ask myself three basic questions: Does it make sense? Does it supply a solution to the problem? And do I have factual information to back up what I am saying? I remember in a meeting two years ago, the vice principal was sitting next to me and she kept looking at me to say something, but I wouldn't. Even the principal looked up as if to say "Mr. Wilson would you please say something NOW?" So finally I did and it made sense. I could see that ninety-percent of the staff around the table went into a moment of shock that a Black man made sense.

Anyway, in this past meeting, a group was coming in to do group counseling with our "tough" population. Well we got on the name of the program and I made a suggestion not to call it a certain name that was suggested. Well someone in the meeting said "We should call it the How to be a Thug group." Everyone kind of snickered but me. I looked at her as if to say "I didn't find that funny." *Are you calling Black boys thugs because of what you see on television?* She knew I was pissed, but I just suggested a new title that made sense and they are actually using it.

As the meeting progressed the vice principal was asking the group for their opinion. I didn't say a word, but when I did say something, it made sense. I could see the other counselors were getting agitated because of their mannerisms and comments. I just laughed and began writing up a program that I want to implement for the summer time for student athletes. We got to the part where we have to draft up a permission slip for the program. Now let me just say I have written hundreds of permission slips. Why? Because I was in charge of so many programs that required me to develop a permission slip. As we began planning the vice principal looked at me and I gave my opinion, "We should keep the permission slip short and sweet, very descriptive and to the point. Eight times out of ten the parents might not read it and just sign it." I gave a number of suggestions because no one was saying anything.

One of the counselors decided to downplay my suggestion, "I think by saying that we may be misleading…" What? Has she ever written a permission slip before? Has she ever dealt with this population?

One of the biggest problems with the school system today is that we have educated, but uneducated people. They are knowledgeable when it comes to books and theory, but they lack the knowledge of working with a difficult population and when they can't do it they begin to form and say stereotypical things about the student(s). My answer is: GET OUT OF THE PROFESSION!

I must stay focused and on task. I'm venting now on paper. I'm pissed right now. You know I believe in the Bible and I attend church regularly, (I am a PK [Preacher's Kid] so what do you expect?). The Bible talks about anger, like in the Book of James it says "My dear brothers… everyone should be quick to listen, slow to speak and slow to become angry…" Well, I'm not trying to hear that right now!

Tuesday, April 15, 2008

Yes, it's another day where I do not feel like being here. We have a one session day. It's not a half day; we just get out two hours and fifteen minutes early. I am kind of tired. I worked out hard in the gym and my body is drained, therefore, I am going home and relax, or maybe do some work in my yard. We have approximately ten weeks left until the end of school and I can't wait. Nothing really happened yesterday with my students so I laid low in my office and did paperwork. Surprisingly, one of the counselor's came into my office and actually held a small conversation with me. Okay Jesus, what are you trying to tell me? Oh well, I put on my "Mr. Bojangles" smile and continued with the conversation. I am not a mean person. I am moody, but I am not mean. I guess I don't want people to judge me by the pigmentation of my skin, but judge me on my character, integrity, and my personality. Sound familiar? Oh yeah, I must share this. I had a teacher bring down a note written by one of my "drama" students. My definition of a "drama student" is one who cannot separate themselves, and often creates unnecessary and chaotic situations in any setting. Of course in my school it is ninety-percent female! Anyway, she wrote me a letter and here is what she gave me (I included the language, punctuation, and spelling of the words she wrote):

Dear Mr. Wilson

There's this new girl that is getting on my nerves. she is always all up on my cuzin Jake, the 8th grader. I was in the hall will my cuz and she was there, and I asked her if she was the new girl, and she said yes with a nasty additude. I was like to not give me adiditude because I haven't nothing to her.

Okay, when I have a session with her the first thing we are going to talk about is being attentive in Language Arts class. Second, does she realize how she gets on my nerves? Third, spelling is a problem! CUZIN + ADDITUDE + ADIDITUDE = HUH? Also, is this a sentence: *I was like to not give me adiditude because I haven't nothing to her?* WHAT? Somebody translate that for me please. Maybe she meant "I asked her not to give me attitude because I didn't do anything to her."

The Mis-Education of Middle School Students! That's a great book title. *The Young, The Dumb, and The Stupid!* That's a great soap opera. *Ultimate Stupidity!* That's a movie.

Well the homeroom bell rang and I have a parent coming in for a Parent/ Teacher conference. Here comes the lip service! Peace for now… I will probably be back before the day is over.

8:40 a.m.

I was just out in the hallway because I like to show my face and have fun with the kids. Of course one thing about being the only brother is you gain popularity especially with the students. To top it off, I love to dress "snazzy." Okay definition: "Snazzy" – dressing professionally with a little flair. One teacher said I look like a "sports star"! I think what the students like is that I have earrings, in both ears! Why do I wear them you may ask. Well for two reasons: One, it's a fashion statement for me, and two, because I want to. Many people think it is unprofessional. No, it's unprofessional to come to work and not do anything. It's unprofessional to talk "ghetto" at work. It's unprofessional to come in dressed like you are going to a cookout, (yes it has happened here). It's unprofessional to work in a school and not care about the students or certain students.

One, I know what I am doing, I do it and I do above and beyond my duties. I am the sixth grade counselor but I see seventh and eighth graders too. If I walk into any classroom the students would know me. Even when new students come in I would go up to them and say, "Hey you're new here, what is your name?" They would tell me their name. Then I would say, "Well I am Mr. Wilson…"

"Yeah I know," they would say.

One Black female student started laughing one time. "I know you're Mr. Wilson."

"Wow, how did you know and this is your second day here?"

"Everyone tells me if I need to talk to come to you because you know what's going on…" I get that response a lot; however, I direct students to their counselor and encourage them to speak with their counselor first and if they definitely need to speak to me I do it in the hallway. I try not to cause any friction.

Many counselors get caught up into "He's mine, she's mine." Whatever! My mentality is to find the person who can assist this student if they do not want to speak to me. These kids need HELP! They already have parents and guardians arguing over them at home, why should they come to school and see the same thing?

Anyway, my parent arrived. Oh she had a "shocked" facial expression. Remember I talked about that earlier in my journal? Oh well, she'll get over it.

12:30 p.m.

Thirty minutes to go and I am out of here. I saw my student who wants to be a biologist. I researched some information for him about going into a career in biology. I told him that anything he wants to do he can do, just to stay focused. I also had a kid who was upset about another student who was always asking him to fight. He said I didn't fix the problem. Whoa... I am not Bob the Builder! I told him to calm down. I just told him that I will alert the vice principal and go from there.

Ladies and gentlemen, we do not "fix" problems as counselors. We assess them and make referrals, (referrals being a phone call to the parent, a note to the Vice Principal, Parent/teacher conferences, and/or a referral to a community agency). Parents, stop thinking we are "parents" to your child. If I were a parent to some of these kids around here, I think I would be under investigation from DYFS! Some days I wish I could walk up and down the hall with my belt in my hand. I'll pop 'em even if they say something stupid like "Africa is a state." POP! Stop being dumb and read a book!

Just a little humor there. I am out of here but I'll be back tomorrow.

Wednesday, April 16, 2008

Well I am the first one in the office and for the first time in a while I am sleepy. I have been waking up during the night thinking about coming to work. That's bad, but most of the time I am thinking about funny stuff, especially with the students.

Like yesterday, I forgot to mention, the same student I mentioned earlier who was going to take a teacher to court, came up to me. "Mr. Wilson I want to file a complaint!" he said looking over the top of his glasses again.

"Against whom? Yourself?" I responded.

"No, Ms. *Bookman*!"

"Hey I am going to count to three and if you don't leave I am getting my lawyer and filing a complaint against you!" I said while laughing. He couldn't help it, he started to laugh but he still refused to go to class. I know you're not supposed to grab kids or put your hands on them, so I grabbed his hoodie and led him into class. "Ms. *Bookman* I think you lost someone and I am here to return him!" He had this big grin on his face.

He LOVES the attention! He likes to make a spectacle in front of the class. The entire sixth grade knows him. There's another sixth grader that craves everyone's attention. He has ADHD and guess what? You guessed it… the meds don't work! One day he came bouncing down the hall, "Hey Mr. Wilson. What's good homie?" he said showing his pearly whites.

"Put your hand down and use it to pick that booger hanging from your nose. Do you look at yourself before you walk out of the house?" I asked with a firm, straight face. "And for the record, I am not your 'homie'! Say that to your father or your uncle!"

"Why you gotta be all mean, Mr. Wilson?" he asked looking totally goofy.

I shouted, "SO YOU CAN LEAVE ME ALONE! But that's not going to happen is it?"

"Nope," he said as he turned to open his locker. I just walked down the hall shaking my head.

I try to be funny with the kids and joke and laugh with them. To me it's a form of connection, but they also know that there is a serious side to me and I constantly remind them that I am not their friend or buddy. That's what parents need to do. Stop this "I am your friend" stuff! Students have friends in school and on the playground!

One day a student in the eighth grade said to me, "Mr. Wilson you not matching today. Is there a reason why you're not matching?"

"Is there a reason why your teeth match your shirt, bright yellow? Do you understand that yellow teeth contribute to halitosis?" I said with a confused look on my face.

"Ooooooo Mr. Wilson tryin' to crack on somebody!"

"No there is a difference between 'cracking' and telling the truth!" I exclaimed.

I heard one student say "C'mon and preach!" I just started laughing because she and I always talk about church but she's always cussing and talking back to teachers! It's funny. Many of the students can identify with me when it comes to church. I was walking down the hallway and a group of students were standing next to the lockers. I said to one student, "*Kyle*, I see you are still acting up."

"No I am not Mr. Wilson. I saved!" He replied while putting his hands in the air like he was praising God. All of a sudden a group of students started shouting, "Hallelujah Mr. Wilson!!"

"You guys need to stop playing with Jesus before he strikes you down with lightning." I said while laughing.

"He ain't gonna strike me down. Why? 'Cause I'm saved!" *Kyle* replied as he started doing a dance like he was in church. Again, the rest of the group started clapping and dancing in the middle of the hallway. I just laughed and walked away.

Well the bell rang and I have to get prepared for Student of the Month. This is where sixth grade teachers select twelve students each month and we give them pizza, ice cream and a certificate and they have lunch with the principal in the conference room. Peace and love for now.

1:10 p.m.

I do not like the way some of the teachers treat students. Now I just saw a student in the office and two teachers had an issue with her. However, four more teachers decided to jump in and put their two cents in. Hello? If you back a kid against the wall they are going to come out swinging! If a student refuses to do what I ask I do not argue back and forth with them, I give them options.

For instance, a classroom teacher called the office and asked me to come to her classroom. When I arrived she had a difficult student who would not leave the class. "Mr. Wilson *Pete* is refusing to leave my room and I am trying to teach. He is being disruptive and rude to the class and myself."

The student said very loudly, "Mr. Wilson ain't going to do nothing! You ain't gonna put your hands on me!"

I said to the teacher "You may continue class while I whisper to Mr. *Pete*. Thanks!" So I walked over to his desk and kneeled down beside him and whispered,

"You're right I am not going to touch you. I can't, it's against the law. However, I am going to give you two options. Option one is when I leave you follow me to my office and we talk about this. Option two is I leave. You stay, while I come back with Detective Walters, who is my fraternity brother, who will arrest you and your mother will have to come and pick you up from a holding cell in the detention center where the Blood members will constantly kick your behind until your mother comes, which won't be until after 5pm because I am going to just happen to forget her number until 6pm! Your choice little brother." I turned and waved to the teacher and started down the hallway.

Suddenly I hear, "Man I hate this school, ya'll make me sick! I should've just stayed in class…"

I quickly interrupted, "But you didn't because you know the outcome. So you can talk all you want as long as you follow me!" I don't argue with kids, that's a waste of time and energy. I try not to let kids get to me. These kids have no respect, no manners, nothing! Some do, but it's a few.

Anyway, I want to express what's on my mind right now. Sometimes I feel like I don't belong here. Many people say, "They need you there… to see a Black man's face that is educated…" No they don't. Parents, staff, and students know that a lot of Black men are educated; some people just refuse to recognize it. A lot of staff members don't want to hear that I may know more than they do. For example, I HATE doing a session with another counselor in the room. Sometimes I feel they have to jump in every time I try and counsel the students like I am ineffective or something. What is it? They don't trust my counseling skills? Maybe someone out there has the answers. If you do, please let me know what it is, PLEASE? They don't like it when

Black men challenge them; and if I do, then it's a problem, "He's not a team player," "He shows a lot of hostility."

Again today I had to keep busy because I felt invisible. My sister often tells me to "Just sit there and get a paycheck... so what if no one speaks to you..." But for me it's different. Black men must be very careful in the workplace. You can't stare, don't joke, don't play around, don't flirt, don't tell jokes, keep it straight business. But you know, I wish I had someone that I could trust and vent to in my office from time to time. I don't have anyone. It's frustrating sometimes. That's the downfall about working here.

I must remember what my ninth grade football coach said to me in a game, "Richard, just suck it up and keep going!" Yeah, I played football in ninth grade, but got hit one good time and my career was over! I feel anywhere an educated Black man goes we are going to be challenged with the worst kind of stereotypical racism. We will be associated with what people see on television, the news, BET (Bafoon Entertainment Television), or any media source that consistently portrays us in a negative light. I have to go because I am getting frustrated... I should just leave early and not care what happens. Just take my stuff and go!

Thursday, April 17, 2008

Man, I woke up with an attitude. I couldn't even take the spin class at the gym. I just ran a mile and did some arm exercises and came home. If it wasn't so late in the school year, I would've taken a mental health day. I am so tired and sleepy again. A teacher came in this morning and asked me if one of her students was in here yesterday.

"Yup."

"What did he say?" she asked.

I just looked at her. "Nothing. He filled out an incident report and he went into his counselor's office. Mr. *Chapman* brought him in here."

"Why?" asking out of frustration.

"Ramble, ramble, ramble…" Does she realize my mind is somewhere else? Does she realize I am not listening because all she wants to do is complain? Hello, I am not listening! She finally left to go and speak with his counselor. I only try to deal with sixth grade teachers because I want to stay on top of the sixth grade.

I don't know how I truly feel today. There's just a blank space. I don't know if I am angry, frustrated, just tired, or what? Do I want to be angry? I want to just get up and quit. I want to go home and just relax! I wish I could do that. Sometimes I just want to be by myself. Sometimes I just want people to leave me alone. Sometimes I just get in a "funk." I just had coffee, now I am chugging down a Red Bull. I gotta perk up, I gotta start moving! Anyway, let me get to work and hopefully the day will get better. Hopefully…

12:00 p.m.

Why can't our young Black men learn what to do and what not to do? We had to send a young man home because he got kicked out of ISS AGAIN! (ISS = In School Suspension). He just can't keep his mouth shut. Now I do believe a lot of teachers do not know how to respond to Black students because they believe what they see on the news. The teacher asked him to remove his gum. "I don't have no gum!" he shouted.

"Well why are you chewing?" she responded.

"I ain't chewing nothing d***!"

"I don't need your smart remarks or I will send you out."

"Well send me out I don't care!"

"Well then get out I don't care," she responded. A piece of advice, don't go back and forth with a child or it will frustrate you.

Wait a minute, two eighth grade girls, *Tatiana* and *Jameera*, came in to talk. I call *Tatiana* and *Jameera* my "two long lost daughters I never had" because that's how much they WORK MY NERVES! I really like them though because their fathers don't spend that much time with them so I feel slightly obligated.

"What do you want?" I exclaimed to *Jameera*. "But wait, before we get started I just want you to know that last week you had an attitude and wouldn't speak, that's wrong!"

"I know Mr. Wilson..." *Jameera* said.

"I'm not finished. You need to check yourself because we are all Black in here and the ghetto can come out behind closed doors, difference is I get paid!"

"Okay dag, Mr. Wilson. Look Mr. Wilson, we need a job..." *Jameera* says while her glasses are falling off her nose.

"Yea Mr. Wilson!" *Tatiana* exclaimed.

"First, I do not know why you two are so loud. Whisper! First get your working papers, then go to the mall and see if they will hire a fourteen year old student."

"Mr. Wilson how we gonna get to the mall? Huh?" *Jameera* asks with a slight attitude.

"Uh.. the bus?"

"The bus!" she shouts, "I ain't catchin' no bus!"

"First *Jameera* stop using double negatives. Second, I guess you're not catching any bus unless it's short and yellow, right?" I said jokingly.

"That's right!" *Jameera* said with pride. Wow. That joke just went over her head. Sometimes that girl is two clowns short of a full circus!

"Mr. Wilson, you gonna help us get a job or what? We should babysit girl." *Tatiana* said to *Jameera*.

"Babysit? I wouldn't trust ya'll with my kids that I don't even have!" I said.

"Here go Mr. Wilson with the jokes again." *Tatiana* said while twisting her mouth up in the air.

Suddenly, in walked a teacher and just interrupted. "Hey *Jameera* I thought you and *Tatiana* were coming to see me?" she said.

The teacher decided to sit in my office and join in, having **NEVER** come this way let alone grace her presence in my counseling domain.

"Just get out and let us finish talking!" is what I wanted to say, however, I told her to "Please, take them to your room." I have to keep it professional. I was tired of them complaining and just talking about absolutely nothing.

I don't know if I mentioned this before but my first year I received no help or advice on how things worked in my school. They didn't go over anything with me; I had to learn everything on my own! All the teachers and everyone else were waiting to see how I was going to handle this job not having any teacher or school experience. Well our first meeting came in May. That's right, May. At the end of the school year! What did they want to talk about? I can remember it as clear as day.

We started the meeting and the other counselors gave each other kudos on the work they had done like I was doing nothing all school year. Then they spoke about eighth grade scheduling, which I don't do. I appeared to be paying attention and taking notes when actually I was writing and drawing pictures. Then suddenly one of the counselors said, "Rich you are doing an excellent job with sixth grade and I know the kids love you, but we are trying to keep the traffic down in the office and I know you have a lot of kids in your office…"

I interrupted, "Yes I know. I don't call those students down, they just come in. I tell them they have to have a pass and usually I go and get the vice principal." Why didn't anyone stop them before they got to my office? After the meeting I was pissed like I am right now. Every time I think about my first year I get pissed off because I had to learn everything on my own. It was made clear that no one in that office was going to train me. I actually heard someone say, "He's going to have to learn on his own…" After hearing that, I had to show them that I could do it.

It's funny, Black men are ridiculed for every little thing, but when we perform our job right, we are the best at what we do with no recognition. I believe Black men can survive anything, because we have! If we read and study our history as African Americans in America, one can conclude that we have taken the worst of the worst! Today, we are the most loved and the most hated!

It will be five years in September and I have taken and done a lot for the school. I don't do it for the glory; I do it for the kids! So you know what… Naw I can't say it. Oops, I gotta go.

Oh no! It's the same student who cries every seventh period. Watch, I am going to walk out there with a pass and he is going to start crying more because he needs to take his crying behind to Language Arts. Hold on…

Boy was he putting it on. Snot and all. I said to him, "You can blow a bubble from the snot in your nose and breath like it was 110 degrees in here and you had on a snow suit but you are GOING back to class." Now you may say, "what if he had a real issue?" He didn't because when I asked him he told me something totally off base which is not worth mentioning. Oh well, he is walking .5 MPH back to class. Hey, as long as he is going back.

2:35 p.m.

I just had two of my sixth grade students in here. Two Black female students; one is too loud and the other one is very quiet. Both of them are very smart. "Mr. Wilson what did you have to talk to me about? Huh? Huh? What did you have to talk to me about? What? What I do? I ain't do nothing…" she said a mile-a-minute. The other student was standing there very quietly.

"*Mary* you didn't do anything. I forgot what I had to tell you…"

"Then why did you call my name down the hall?" she asked as she rolled her eyes to the top of her head. Then I noticed a note sticking out of her pocket and I held my hand out. She knew what that meant. "Mr. Wilson, I can't give you the note! It's not mine! I can't Mr. Wilson! I can't!" she said. I just looked at her as she reached in her pocket and gave me the note reluctantly.

As I opened it I could smell the profanity. As soon as I opened it the first word I saw was "Fuk…" These kids can't even spell cuss words right. Then

I saw the word I hate the most: "Nigga." Why? "YOU WROTE THIS?" I asked very firmly.

"No!" she said almost half scared because they know how I feel about that word. Then I looked and saw who wrote the letter. It was a white female sixth grader who SWEARS she is Black. What she doesn't know is that the Black female students she follows everywhere don't want her to hang around them.

Well I guess I have to call the girl down and first talk to her about the use of profanity, second, her spelling errors, and third, that she CANNOT use that word! It's offensive. And I told both students who were in my office, "You should be ashamed of yourselves! You are letting her or anyone else use this word. Be mindful of where this word came from. Forget what rappers or the streets say, listen to what MR. WILSON SAYS! STOP USING IT!"

Friday, April 18, 2008

Whew! It was a busy morning. It's almost third period. I had to talk to a homeroom about scheduling, talk to five students, conference with a parent, and sweep my office because of this ant problem. Aww man, but you know what? I drank two Red Bulls and I feel alright. I am bouncing off of walls right now just like the kids.

I have to say this, I came in angry this morning because I thought about the teacher who hit me in the head with a stack of envelopes. The incident took place last year. She told the vice principal that she was just "Playing around…" That woman doesn't know me! See I am getting angry again. Then I walked into an office where I am the odd man out.

Then it happened… A student came in and gave me a flower for no reason! I was shocked! "Mr. Wilson are you here?" one of the counselors's said, "a student needs to see you." I looked at the clock and hung my head and said to myself "*Here we go… what now?*" She walked in the door.

"Hey Mr. Wilson, I just came in to give you this." I looked and it looked like a pink tulip. "I picked it from my yard."

"Oh wow," I said with a surprised look on my face. "I wasn't expecting this. *Julie*, you brought this at the right time. You cheered me up. Thank you for thinking of me." Then she walked out.

You know, I believe God sends people in your time of need. I personally believe that there are angels who walk the Earth but we don't know who they are. There may be some in this school... Psych! It's definitely demons in here! I crack myself up. But I do believe there are angels around us. Do I believe the kid who gave me a flower is an angel? Uh... NO! She was just cussing a kid out the other day and she is involved in SO MUCH DRAMA! Well, the bell is about to ring and I gotta get some work done. Peace for now.

1:50 p.m.

Oh wow! Since lunch it seemed like every student wanted to talk to me. I didn't get a break. Oh my goodness!

I had one student who came down from a test because he was "pissed off" at students who don't even attend our school. "Mr. Wilson, you don't understand! People piss me off! I just had to leave the class!" he said.

"Hey *Ken*, I am pissed off too but you do not see me leaving work. We have to learn how to deal with being angry."

"You don't get it," he said with a big smile on his face, "Mr. Wilson, I pissed off!"

I responded back to him with the intentions to make him laugh, "Students piss me off all the time. Like when students refuse to get a haircut and get pissed off at people who don't attend our school..." He started laughing because he looked like he was leading a student sit-in protesting every barber in the United States.

Then I had a student who has serious emotional issues. SERIOUSLY! I couldn't joke with him. I had to pull out my counseling techniques for him. He eventually calmed down and went to class. Then I had *Jameera* and *Tatiana* in my office. *Jameera* and *Tatiana* are the students I had yesterday who wanted jobs but didn't want to catch the bus. They got on my last nerve.

I am tired right now. I need a Red Bull. I should just go to the store and buy one.

Then a teacher came in, (not one of the sixth grade teachers), who I think is scared to look me in the eyes. I just stare at her as if to say "C'mon man look at me... I'm Black!" Anyway, I am ready to go home. I just had a kid walk in my office and he was "fake" crying. I just stared at him. He looked at me, "What Mr. Wilson?" he shouted. I just kept staring. He put the book up to cover his face and tried to peek. I just kept staring. Soon he started to laugh. I just reached for my passes and gave him a pass to class. All he wanted was a pass because he was late.

I told him, "Next time just come in and admit that you're late for class and you want a pass. Then I will throw you out." I also had a young female sixth grader that was crying out in the hallway. I told her to come in and we'd talk about what was bothering her. She stated that another sixth grader hated her and she didn't understand why.

"Mr. Wilson he hates me and I haven't done anything to him. We were never friends, even in elementary school," she stated while fighting back the tears.

"Do you want to be his friend," I asked.

"NO!" she said.

"Is he picking on you, calling you names, is he bullying you?"

"No..."

Then why in the world are you crying? This is what I said in my mind! I brought him down and we worked it out. Quite frankly, I think they like each other. They both left my office with smiles on their faces. My wife asked me one time if I would ever be a high school counselor. I told her no, because in the middle school, in my opinion, you do more counseling. I like that. Plus if a student raises up to hit me in high school I am going to proceed to kick his... Well I would restrain him!

Anyway, the time is drawing nigh to leave this place. Hallelujah! I made it through another week. There are nine more weeks to go until summer break. I am going to Jamaica and I can't wait. Well I am not worrying about that now; I AM READY TO GET OUT OF THIS PLACE! I'm drained...

Monday, April 21, 2008

It has begun! It is Monday morning and I have been on the run since 8:00 a.m. In a span of forty-five minutes, I have seen eight students. Good gracious! I had four sixth grade African American female students who came to me in the hallway. "Mr. Wilson, Mr. Wilson! We need to talk to you!" they shouted.

"You have a pass to come see me?" I said as I stayed focused on making it to my office in one piece.

"No we was looking all over for you!"

"First of all, it's we were looking... Pay attention in Language Arts class," I said. "And I am not available to students who don't have passes." They kept following me and talking loudly about nothing, they were making excuses to come and see me. One kept asking me if her eye was red. Another said she needed a schedule because she lost hers. The other two said they had an issue with a sixth grade boy which I solved three weeks ago.

"Get in my office right now!" I shouted as they looked at me with bubbled eyes. "Don't sit down because this is going to be quick. I am not in a counselor's role right now; I am your 'play daddy'! You will not prance around in the halls and expect me to give you passes, understand me?"

"Yes," they said while looking at me in shock.

"All of you didn't want anything, just passes so you wouldn't be late to class! I am not bailing you out next time... STOP USING ME!" I exclaimed as I banged my fist on the desk. One girl went to sit down. "STAND UP I'M NOT FINISHED!" I shouted. I just stared at them for thirty seconds. You could hear a cotton ball drop on the carpet.

"We sorry... I mean we're sorry Mr. Wilson." I reached in my desk and pulled out my pink passes. They grinned as I smiled back at them.

"You know, I am sooooo glad I don't have any daughters!"

56

"We your daughters," one of the girls said.

"NO I DON'T THINK SO!" I said. I was getting irritated because one of the girls kept asking me if her eye was red for the umpteenth time! "If you ask me that one more time... here are your passes."

"Mr. Wilson I still need a schedule. I don't know where I am going," one of the girls whined.

"Well I suggest you peek into every class and ask the teacher 'is this my class?' Now go and you are banned from bothering me for the rest of the day."

"Bye Mr. Wilson," they all said in unison.

"Don't speak to me!" I had to laugh when I sat at my desk. That episode was enough to drain me; but I am just getting started.

I was also asked to call a parent of an unruly seventh grade student. This is where I go above and beyond my job. No one wants to call this mother because she gets nasty, (I think I introduced you to her earlier in my book). Anyway, I think his counselor is scared to call. If the vice principal didn't ask me to call, I wouldn't call. Peace for now...

11:45 a.m.

Oh wow! Lunch time is always "drama" time! I actually had ten students follow me around the cafeteria. Ten! For what? Two of them kept tapping me on the shoulder. I just ignored them and kept walking. We went outside for our ten minute recess and three more joined the group. Is this the Mummer's Parade? One of the students was jumping up and down in front of me. Three other students kept cursing because they thought their issues were more important than any one else's issues. One girl kept telling me she had a boyfriend in the seventh grade. Nerve wrecking! I just stood there thinking about how many days we had left of school! I am glad lunch is over. Whew!

Tuesday, April 22, 2008

As I am getting ready for my journal entry, I just happened to look out my window. There were two groups of students gathered on the school lawn. One Black, one white. My attention was immediately drawn to the Black students. Why? I think the media has us brainwashed into thinking if a group of young Black people are together something is bound to happen. Well, I must say, there were two vicious fights broadcasted over the internet that gained national attention and they weren't Black students.

I have to change my way of thinking and their way of acting. When I see a group of them in the hall I step right into the middle of their circle and say "Now, you know you are going to draw attention to yourselves. Why don't you break up into small groups of two or three because you are probably going to talk about the same thing anyway."

I had an invisible moment this morning so I went into the hallways with the students. At least with them I am recognized. They love me and I love them too no matter how they act. I was out in the halls and one of my hyper students came up to me talking a mile a minute. "Mr. Wilson, Mr. Wilson, Mr. Wilson I need to talk to you! Are you listening?" she said while following me up the hall.

"Okay get a pass and we can talk," I responded.

"No I need to speak to you now! I need to talk now Mr. Wilson. Right now!" I mistakenly tapped her with my arm when I went to turn the corner.

"OOOO Mr. Wilson, I'm calling DYFS!" she yelled.

"Good. Then maybe they can take me out of this place!" I turned and said to her with a huge smile on my face.

"No that's okay; I wanna talk to you... Right now Mr. Wilson! Please?" So I spoke with her and guess what? She didn't want anything. She just wanted to be late to her first period class. UNBELIEVABLE! I have a parent to call so peace and love for now.

10:25 a.m.

I was cleaning out my bag and I found this poem I wrote about our youth
that I want to share:

Separate and Unequal, No balance

Describes the Youth colored Ebony and Ivory

When is change gonna come?

Is what I ask myself as I gaze down

The dimly lit tunnel of freedom

The exchange of books for guns and pockets laced with chump change

and a mindset of invincibility

Makes it easy for change not to come

What about the 10% proclaimed by W.E.B.?

It's like comparing a dime to a plethora of thousands of dollar bills

The mis-education of the uneducated becomes a norm as the thirst of having role

models switches from prominent Black figures to the figures on BET, what now?

Is there any hope for change? Or the only change we have is the change our

homeless brothers and sisters beg for...

As far as I can see, change will never come

As the bottom continues to look muddy in this river of life.

Thank you. Thank you. No autographs please. Well it's almost time for
my lunch duty. I have to get mentally prepared for it. And I am off to the
races!

1:00 p.m.

I am observing a classroom because I want to document a student's behavior.
Sometimes I do that as a counselor to make myself visible to the students.
The class is large and packed with behavior problems and mouths running
like cars with endless gas! I walk in and immediately I am the center of
attention getting questions from students that have nothing to do with class.

There are twenty seven students in the class and at least four are serious "nerve wreckers." That's really all you need. The teacher actually let's one student sit on the radiator because he behaves more appropriately.

They are taking a quiz right now and you can tell which students did not study. I know whose parents I am going to call after this class! Oh my goodness, two minutes into the quiz and a boy is finished already. F! One of the students just asked me what I was typing. "Mr. Wilson," he whispers, "What you typing?"

"Fifty reasons why you should get an F!" I whispered back. He just smiled and turned around. I have so much respect for teachers since I started working here. They should be rewarded with three months off!

After the quiz, the little boy on the radiator started singing. He has ADHD – **A**in't **D**one **H**omework in **D**ays! He never does his homework! Now I have a student singing in back of me. Now I have a boy talking to himself to the right of me. These kids are crazy, but I have to help them.

There is a boy in the front of the room rocking from side to side really quickly. I have two drummers, a paper airplane maker, a sleeper, three day dreamers, and a student who keeps raising his hand to answer a question but his responses are all wrong. He's not discouraged because there is his hand again! The boy from the radiator just "pimp-walked" his way to get another piece of paper to take notes. Umm, where is his notebook? I just gave him an "I wish I was your daddy so I can take my belt off" look. I can't believe the student beside me tried to throw a paper airplane to the student next to me! His parents are coming in tomorrow. Wow!

Radiator Boy is having serious issues. He is stretched across the radiator as if he were watching TV. Mercy! That other boy got another answer wrong. I think some of them are trying to "show off" because I am here. The student sitting next to me keeps making noises that are indescribable. Now he is tapping me with a pen and continuously calling my name. "Mr. Wilson, Mr. Wilson, Mr. Wilson, Mr. Wilson, Mr. Wilson..."

"Didn't you just fail the quiz?" I asked trying to get him to stop calling my name. Radiator Boy just got an answer wrong which was on the overhead projector all he had to do was look up. Wow! Teachers, God bless you!

Wednesday, April 23, 2008

It is 12:35 p.m. and my day was filled with meetings and student issues. The immediate student issue I have now is a new game in the air. If one male student asks another male student to hold out his hand and he cuffs it, they have to hit a girl on the butt. What? Three girls were hit so far so I am doing an investigation. So far I have two culprits. They were immediately reported to the principal.

I met with some teachers today to discuss students. The same names keep popping up in our meetings. You know I have been inspired to write another book entitled *What a Parent Should Know about Middle School Children*. Yes parents, your child will lie to you. Yes parents, your child will have a girlfriend or boyfriend. Yes parents, your child may have a MySpace page you don't know about. Parents are a trip! I really believe that some parents have "missed the boat"! Some parents, or guardians, are very supportive. I spoke to one grandmother and she told me "If you have ANY problems with *Lori*, call me and I will come up there and tear her ----- up! And she knows I mean it because I did it to her father!"

Thursday, April 24, 2008

Yesterday was a very, very busy day for me. I can't even begin to tell you. Four meetings, a parent conference, kids begging to see me, observing a class, individual counseling sessions, a session with my intern... and the list goes on. I like it like that because the day goes by faster for me. Today, I have five parents to call and an intensive inpatient program who wants to take us to court.

Okay, case scenario: A student transfers to our school and only attends for two weeks. The student is admitted to an intensive inpatient program because of suicidal ideations. We receive a letter from DYFS stating she will not be returning to our school. The program calls me and says the girl needs a tutor and our school should provide the services. I tell the case manager that we received a letter from DYFS stating she would not be returning; in addition, I spoke with the student's DYFS worker and she stated that we are not responsible for the tutoring. I received a phone call from the case manager and she stated that we are responsible and they are prepared to take it to court because she has not had any tutoring. For all the professors, psychologists, educators, counselors, answer this question for me: Are we responsible for tutoring even with the letter from DYFS stating she will not be returning to our school? I am definitely taking the class "Education and the Law" at Rider University next year. I have to stay on top of "the game." I don't know where I am getting the money from because I am broke! I am so broke a bum gave me change!

Anyway, I have a workshop in the afternoon and one of my colleagues from another school won't be there. Well I'll become the invisible man. I am purposely going late so I can stand in the back. I am leaving at 3:15! That's what our contract states. I looked at the workshop sheet and we have to attend from 1:30-3:15 p.m. Let me get started early on my work. Peace for now.

1:00 p.m.

Ahhhh! The students are gone and my colleagues went to a workshop. No, I didn't go because I have some work to catch up on. Actually, I am waiting to do a conference call between DYFS and the intensive inpatient program I mentioned earlier. Today was "take your child to work day", so some of the staff had their children at work. Since I don't have any children I decided to adopt two students in the school as my kids. Wow! Did they go overboard. I adopted an eleven year old African American male sixth grader with ADHD,

(Radiator Boy who I mentioned earlier), and a thirteen year old Hispanic female eighth grader. Boy that was a mistake. All day I kept hearing, "Hey Daddy! Hey Daddy!"

I said to the sixth grader, "This is why I don't have kids!" But I can see that adopting them for the school day made their day. I was happy to see them smiling all day.

Friday, May 2, 2008

It's been a while since I visited my journal because we just finished a week of standardized testing. Our seventh and eighth graders were taking the NJASK (New Assessment of Skills and Knowledge). I personally believe our society puts too much emphasis on test scores (whether it's the NJASK or the SAT). I believe those standardized tests are culturally biased, but that's just my opinion. I must ask, do standardized test scores reveal true academic qualities of a student? What if he or she is an honor roll student but just happens to score poorly on a specific standardized test? Should the student be rejected from college? Or placed in a Basic Skills class? The flip side is you may have a student who is low academically; however, he or she has a "magic pencil" and scores high on a standardized test. Oh well, that's the way society works, right?

I want to vent right now. I am disturbed at an incident that happened at my school involving a Black male student who was voted by teachers to receive an award; however, some people had a problem with it. I am not going to give details, however let me share this. In my opinion, it all points to how people stereotype young Black males. If you wear a wave cap, with big clothes, a long gold or silver necklace, and speak a certain way you're labeled as a "thug". That is not the case with some students and many of our Black male students. It is unfortunate that there are some Black male students who wear their pants half off of their behind, wear the wave cap, and have a non-caring attitude regarding their lives. Do not categorize all of "us" that way. The reason that I say "us" is because I am an African American male too.

Sunday, May 4, 2008

It is Sunday evening and I am preparing to go to church but I decided to type in my journal for the last time. The sixth graders have testing so this week should go by pretty quickly. I am sitting here in my den thinking and reflecting on the school year. Sometimes I feel that in certain situations some people believe I don't know what I'm talking about when it comes to working with the students. Sometimes when I give my opinion they look at me as if to say, "You don't know more than me..." I DO know what I am talking about.

I have been in the counseling profession for fifteen years, I had better know something. Oh well.

Thursday, June 05, 2008

It's been a month since my last journal entry. So much has taken place with staff and students. I am sitting here thinking about what I am going to do for the summer. We have TWO WEEKS and school will be OVER! I made it another year. I am sitting here reflecting on this past school year.

There is one major concern I had to deal with during my fourth year. I believe I mentioned this earlier that we as counselors, teachers, and administrators need to know how to approach and deal with certain students. With this generation, getting mad and trying to argue with them is USELESS! If we are in the business of helping our youth we need to know how to talk with them. Seriously, some students you cannot blame for the way they act or react because that is all they know. I feel it is my job to teach them the right way to do certain things so they can have a chance at succeeding in life.

On a funny note, we had the eighth grade Social, (it's like a prom in the middle school). That Monday morning after the social, I stood in the middle of the hallway as the homeroom bell rang and observed a group of eighth grade girls struttin' down the hall like they were superstars.

"Ahhhh" I said to the group of girls who were approaching while looking up in the air as if to say *"I am going to wait until Mr. Wilson speaks to me because I am being GRAND right now."* "I can tell all of you went to the social Friday night."

"Mr. Wilson, how can you tell?" one of the girls said while standing right in front of me with her hand on her hip and a huge ghetto smile.

"Because for the first time all year ya'll FINALLY did something with your hair. I was worried for a while." I said jokingly as I noticed all their lips poking upward. I have to admit, their hair looked really nice and I can tell they were proud. You know, when my students look nice whether they get their hair done or they are dressed up, their attitude changes. I can really talk to them.

"Mr. Wilson, I know my hair looked good, but you ain't gotta make jokes just because you tryin' to grow your hair back." *Karen* said while rolling her eyes.

"That's right Mr. Wilson. I know I look good." *Tatiana* said. You know she is the one I mentioned earlier who wouldn't catch the bus to the mall to get a job.

"No, honestly, you girls look really nice," I said with a half smile. "Now if only your grades can catch up to how you look right now we would be in good shape."

Man, when I mentioned grades they move away from me faster then roaches in light. Those girls have a good heart no matter how much they get on my nerves.

Wait! Remember *Jameera* from earlier in my book? You know, the girl who was dancing with the pizza box? Well she came in my office with Tatiana again really loudly.

"Hey girl don't you know *Mrs. Yarn* tried to give me codes to write." She said with a frustrated voice however with a big smile on her face.

When some students get in trouble sometimes the teachers make them write codes of conduct which includes the school's mission statement. Well, *Jameera* wrote her own codes including her own mission statement. Wow!

"Listen *Tatiana*, these are *Jameera's* codes and mission statement." Jameera said proudly as I sat there on edge waiting to hear this ghetto mission statement that I was sure to get a huge laugh. After reading them I had to list them for you as the reader. Please pay close attention:

JAMEERA'S DISTRICT (like she owns a bunch of schools)
MISSION STATEMENT

1. *Prepare yourselves mentally and physically for the process of being fly.* (Oh My Goodness!)
2. *Demonstrate respect for the sexiest girl ever!*
3. *Take responsibility if you look a hot mess!* (Does she realize this applies to her too?)
4. *Take responsibility for your fakeness.*
5. *If a friend lets you look a mess, smack them!*
6. *Meet the unique requirements of nice dressing.*
7. *Monitor your dressing.* (She is standing in front of me looking like a bag of Skittles! not matching at all!)
8. *Communicate with peers and school personnel about dress related matters.* (I hope we get uniforms!)

Can you see what I go through? If she puts that much energy into her school work, she will have no problem going to college!

Friday, June 6, 2008

I just completed my outreach sessions with the incoming fifth graders. I visited six elementary schools in our district and did a presentation about our middle school. Of course I am worried about one of the elementary schools because it gets a bad rep. Why? Because most of our African American students come from this elementary school and some are low academically or have behavior problems. The issue I have is that they are labeled even before they get here. I hate that! You know, for me that is the life of a Black man. Sometimes we are labeled until we prove ourselves "worthy". I had to prove myself my first year, but you know, that's the way it is so I have to deal with it. Quite frankly, with the way we are portrayed in movies, the news, in the music industry, it is not getting any better.

Tuesday, June 17, 2008

Well I haven't written in my journal since Friday, but it is the LAST day of school for students and my last day "mentally". THANK GOD! I had a group of students in my office early in the morning. I purposely shut my door and pretended I was on the phone with a parent. Did that stop them? NO! They barged right into my office shouting, "Mr. Wilson sign my yearbook! Mr. Wilson, sign my shirt! Mr. Wilson, let me take a picture of you before I leave for the summer!" Even though I felt like a celebrity they still worked my nerves. But hey, I love the children.

Yesterday I played in a charity basketball game at the school and I am sore! I work out everyday, but I still feel sore. Some of the staff played some of the top basketball players in the eighth grade. I played just to stay in shape and because one of the teachers asked me to play.

I was sitting on the bench after I played most of the first half, analyzing my environment. Thoughts of me being the only Black man came to mind and I started getting frustrated. I looked around me and most of the teachers playing had their families there having a good time. My teammates were socializing with them during the game having a good time, but I couldn't. I didn't know anyone. I wasn't introduced to anyone. So what did I do? Yes, I went to tease the kids on the other team because I knew I could get some interaction from them. I felt alone when I came home from the game, like the black sheep. I actually went home and spoke with my wife about it because she could tell I was frustrated. "Honey, what's wrong?" she asked.

"Nothing." I responded. You know it's hard sometimes for Black men to express what is on our minds. We would rather keep it bottled up inside and deal with it ourselves. I truly believe that keeping stuff inside attributes to a lot of Black men's health problems, especially those problems related to stress.

"I know you," she stated while looking at me with piercing eyes. "You got frustrated at work again? What happened?"

"I had one of those 'I am the only brother moments' again. I need to find a school where I can at least feel comfortable fifty percent of the time. Why do I have to go through it?"

"Babe you know God has a plan…"

"Stacey I'm not trying to hear that right now. Can't I just be angry?" I said to her as I shut my eyes while lying on my coach watching the movie *Jumper.*

I believe that we as Black men face many challenges that a lot of other groups do not. **Black men are in a state of emergency**! Now, there are a lot of good Black men out there; however all the media broadcasts are the ones that are locked up, on the street, entertainers, etc. What about the hard working, intelligent brothers out there? Do we get any press? NO! What about the ones who are dedicated family men? What about the ones who try and help youth get out of gangs? What about the "everyday working man" who tries to keep his family together? Broadcast that! I think the media is afraid of what the outcome might be – an insurgence of young Black men doing what is right! Oh well, I am going to keep trying to help our youth in general, our young Black men in particular.

Maybe God put me here at this school for a reason even though sometimes I don't want to go through the challenging times. It doesn't matter where I am, I will always try to connect with our young people. Somebody has to. My father always tells me to pray like it always depends on God and work like it always depends on me; while my mother always gives me that motherly support, (I am a momma's boy). A parent once told me how happy she was I was there because her son always speaks highly of me at home. I had another parent not too long ago who told me the same thing about her son. One is black and one is white. You know what, I figure Black or White, male or female, it doesn't matter; I work with them all and do a good job!

I guess I have to keep holding on. I am going to end it here and finish out the rest of the fourth marking period. I just wanted to give you a glimpse of what I encounter as an African American male guidance counselor. My thoughts, my experiences... On June 20th I will be a free man; at least for the summer. September 4, 2008 is the start of another book.

I had a chance to do an informal interview with two very good friends Mr. Derrick Davis, Vice Principal of 18th Avenue School in Newark, New Jersey and Ms. Melda Grant, Director of School Based Youth Services at Trenton Central High School in Trenton, New Jersey. Both participants have experience working with youth both in and out of the school system. Below is a brief discussion I had with Mr. Davis and Ms. Grant regarding their thoughts and experiences working in the field of education.

For how many years have you been working in the school system?

Davis: Fifteen years
Grant: Five years

This book has two perspectives, my thoughts and feelings and my experiences. What are your personal feelings about working in the school system?

Davis: Let me put it to you this way. Working in the school system would be a lot easier if everyone working in the schools was an advocate of children.
Grant: I share some of the same concerns as Mr. Davis. There is a disconnection between staff and students, understanding their needs, their environment, and their socio-economic status. My concern is that I don't see it getting better. One may even ask is it realistic at this point to expect that public schools can change?
Me: I agree. There is a form of disconnection. I believe schools hire people with the belief that with all their experience or because they

know this or that person they are getting someone who can work with this generation of children. There needs to be a deeper scrutiny on whom schools hire, but sometimes it is all bureaucratic. I don't see the cycle changing.

Davis: I think that public schools can change. One way public schools can change is if you have administrations that monitor their staff to bring about change. Not only monitor their staff but be educational leaders.

Mr. Davis this question is specifically for you. In your fifteen years of working as an African American male in the school system, have you ever felt "invisible?" (I read a passage from Ralph Ellison's book <u>Invisible Man</u>)

Davis: No. I have never felt that way for two reasons. Being an administrator, I have to meet and talk with everyone. Sometimes as a vice principal, when people come to the school I introduce myself but not as the "vice principal." I let them discover who I am. Now your situation is a little different. I am an administrator in a predominately Black school, while you're a guidance counselor in a predominately white school.

Ms. Grant this question is for you. As an African American woman do you think Black men face more challenges, especially psychologically, working in the field of education?

Grant: I believe that education is one the few fields Black men tend to pursue and is in demand, especially in urban areas because of the need to service young Black boys. Black men are not seen in the schools and they need to be!

Me: I know. We need more Black male professionals in our schools, not only for black boys, but for all children. Sometimes all they see is what is on the news... negative publicity.

Grant: ...I went to a workshop were the facilitator, who is an African American male, went into an elementary school to do a workshop and one of the students thought he was Dr. Martin Luther King Jr!

As a guidance counselor in a middle school I try to be visible to all the students. I am in the hallways between classes and in the lunch room. How would you describe your daily interactions with your students?

Davis: I try to be proactive... I don't mind doing lunch duty and playground duty. I get a chance to watch who is interacting with whom, who is doing what. You need to have that connection with the students!

Grant: Being in support services, we interact with students all the time. We must be knowledgeable of student needs. I encourage my staff to be proactive with the students at my school.

One point sticks out in my mind after the interview; I asked if parents should be held accountable for the students' lack of knowledge and behavior problems. Mr. Davis made a very good point. Summarizing his statement, he basically stated that it shouldn't all be placed on the parents, especially in urban districts. Many parents are unable and for some, unwilling to care for their children. Should we just let the children suffer? We all agreed that a lot of parents are not involved with their children; therefore, in my opinion, as educators and advocates for children, we need to take a step up! It does get frustrating at times, but we can't lose sight of why we chose this profession. Now if you are not ready to do that, maybe you should think about a career change!

ABOUT THE AUTHOR

Richard L. Wilson, Jr. grew up in Trenton, NJ. He attended Rowan University where he received a Baccalaureate degree in Communications, with a minor in African American Studies. He continued his studies at Rider University earning a Master's degree in Counseling Services with a certification in School Counseling. Rich just completed his first book entitled The 4th Marking Period: A Memoir of an African American Male Guidance Counselor. He currently resides with his wife Stacey in Westampton, New Jersey.

Visit me on www.myspace.com/richwilsonjr

Email me at jubalentertainment@gmail.com

Printed in the United States
205969BV00001B/379-492/P